CHARACTER AND P

Core concepts in therapy

Series editor: Michael Jacobs

Over the last ten years a significant shift has taken place in the relations between representatives of different schools of therapy. Instead of the competitive and often hostile reactions we once expected from each other, therapists from different points of the spectrum of approaches are much more interested in where they overlap and where they differ. There is a new sense of openness to cross orientation learning.

The series In Search of a Therapist also published by the Open University Press has already contributed in a major way to this process of rapprochement and dialogue, examining the way in which therapists differ or overlap in the way they work with a particular client or presenting set of issues. The next step is to examine theoretical models, and the commonalities and difference in the use of technical concepts, which form the language of psychotherapy.

The Core Concepts in Therapy series compares and contrasts the use of similar terms across a range of the therapeutic models, and seeks to identify where different terms appear to denote similar concepts. Each book is authored by two therapists, each one from a distinctly different orientation; and, where possible, each one from a different continent, so that an international dimension becomes a feature of this network of ideas.

Each of these short volumes examines a key concept in psychological therapy, setting out comparative positions in a spirit of free and critical enquiry, but without the need to prove one model superior to another. The books are fully referenced and point beyond themselves to the wider literature on each topic.

CHARACTER AND PERSONALITY TYPES

Nick Totton
and
Michael Jacobs

Open University Press
Buckingham · Philadelphia

Open University Press
Celtic Court
22 Ballmoor
Buckingham
MK18 1XW

email: enquiries@openup.co.uk
world wide web: www.openup.co.uk

and
325 Chestnut Street
Philadelphia, PA 19106, USA

First Published 2001

A catalogue record of this book is available from the British Library

ISBN   0 335 20639 5 (pb)   0 335 20640 9 (hb)

Library of Congress Cataloging-in-Publication Data
Totton, Nick.
     Character and personality types / Nick Totton and Michael Jacobs.
        p.   cm. – (Core concepts in therapy)
     Includes bibliographical references and index.
     ISBN 0-335-20640-9 – ISBN 0-335-20639-5 (pbk.)
     1. Psychotherapy. 2. Personality. 3. Character. 4. Typology
(Psychology)   I. Jacobs, Michael, 1941. II. Title. III. Series.
RC480.5 .T659 2001
616.89'14 –dc21

                                                                    00-050176

Typeset by Graphicraft Limited, Hong Kong
Printed in Great Britain by The Cromwell Press, Trowbridge

Contents

Series editor's preface

A major aspect of intellectual and cultural life in the twentieth century has been the study of psychology – present, of course, for many centuries in practical form and expression in the wisdom and insight to be found in spirituality, in literature and in the dramatic arts, as well as in arts of healing and guidance, both in the East and West. In parallel with the deepening interest in the inner processes of character and relationships in the novel and theatre in the nineteenth century, psychiatry reformulated its understanding of the human mind, and encouraged, in those brave enough to challenge the myths of mental illness, new methods of exploration of psychological processes.

The second half of the twentieth century in particular witnessed an explosion of interest both in theories about personality, psychological development, cognition and behaviour, as well as in the practice of therapy or, perhaps more accurately, the therapies. It also saw, as is common in any intellectual discipline, battles between theories and therapists of different persuasions, particularly between psychoanalysis and behavioural psychology, and each in turn with humanistic and transpersonal therapies, as well as within the major schools themselves. Such arguments are not surprising, and indeed objectively can be seen as healthy – potentially promoting greater precision in research, alternative approaches to apparently intractable problems, and deeper understanding of the wellsprings of human thought, emotion and behaviour. It is nonetheless disturbing that, for many decades, there was such a degree of sniping and entrenchment of positions from therapists who should have been able to look more closely at their own responses and rivalries. It is as if diplomats had ignored their skills and knowledge and resorted in their dealings with each other to gun-slinging.

The psychotherapeutic enterprise has also been an international one. There were many centres of innovation, even at the beginning – Paris, Moscow, Vienna, Berlin, Zurich, London and Boston, USA – and soon Edinburgh, Rome, New York, Chicago and California saw the development of different theories and therapeutic practice. Geographical location has added to the richness of the discipline, in particular identifying cultural and social differences, and widening the psychological debate to include, at least in some instances, sociological and political dimensions.

The question has to be asked, given the separate developments due to location, research interests, personal differences and splits between and within traditions, whether what has sometimes been called 'psycho-babble' is indeed a welter of different languages describing the same phenomena through the particular jargon and theorizing of the various psychotherapeutic schools? Or are there genuine differences, which may lead sometimes to the conclusion that one school has got it right, while another has therefore got it wrong; or that there are 'horses for courses'; or, according to the Dodo principle, that 'all shall have prizes'?

The latter part of the twentieth century saw some rapprochement between the different approaches to the theory and practice of psychotherapy (and counselling), often due to the external pressures towards organizing the profession responsibly and to the high standards demanded of it by health care, by the public and by the state. It is out of this budding rapprochement that there came the motivation for this series, in which a number of key concepts that lie at the heart of the psychotherapies can be compared and contrasted across the board. Some of the terms used in different traditions may prove to represent identical concepts; others may look similar, but in fact highlight quite different emphases, which may or may not prove useful to those who practise from a different perspective. Other terms, apparently identical, may prove to mean something completely different in two or more schools of psychotherapy.

To carry out this project, it was essential that as many of the psychotherapeutic traditions as possible should be represented in the authorship of the series. To promote both this and the spirit of dialogue between traditions, it also seemed desirable that there should be two authors for each book, each one representing, where practicable, different orientations. It was important that the series should be truly international in its approach and therefore in its authorship.

And that miracle of late twentieth-century technology, the Internet, proved to be a productive means of finding authors, as well as a remarkably efficient method of communicating, in the cases of some pairs of authors, half-way across the world.

This series therefore represents, in a new millennium, an extremely exciting development, one which as series editor I have found more and more enthralling as I have eavesdropped on the drafts shuttling back and forth between authors. Here, for the first time, the reader will find all the major concepts of all the principal schools of psychotherapy and counselling (and not a few minor ones) drawn together so that they may be compared, contrasted and (it is my hope) above all used – used for the ongoing debate between orientations; but more importantly still, used for the benefit of clients and patients who are not at all interested in partisan positions, but in what works, or in what throws light upon their search for healing and understanding.

Michael Jacobs

Preface

The topic of character and personality types is exceptionally suited to a series like the one in which this book appears. It is extremely difficult for the student or interested reader to find their way through the jungle of different typologies that has sprung up in the field of psychotherapy; and even harder for them to find a point of sufficient height above the forest canopy to get their bearings to compare one system with another. This volume attempts to offer such an observation point, together with some possible mappings.

A word of explanation is necessary about the writing of this book. Nick Totton, who was among the first of the authors recruited for the series, made significant contributions to the outline of the series at an early residential meeting of some of the authors at Launde Abbey in Leicestershire, England. From the outset he was keen to undertake this volume, and was initially going to write it with Sean Orford, whose background is not only in psychodynamic therapy but also in Eastern therapies. Unfortunately, Sean had to withdraw because of pressures at work, and although he later returned to the project, found he was limited in the contribution he could make, due to other factors then interfering with his commitment to the series. He has, however, been able to share some of his specialist knowledge with other authors in the series, and has made a major contribution to Chapter 6 in the section on Eastern typologies.

Michael Jacobs replaced Sean when it was clear he could take his contribution no further, in order to help the book to appear on schedule, although it has been Nick who has assembled by far the most material. The task of collating and editing has been both a shared and a productive one.

551555555555155555555551555555555515

Nick would like to thank the following for their very different contributions to this book, some quite specific and some over a period of years: Jim Davis, Em Edmondson, Andrew Samuels and William West. He also wishes to express gratitude to all those whom he has tried to train in post-Reichian character analysis; and to Hélène Fletcher for her profound support.

Nick Totton
Michael Jacobs

CHAPTER 1

Orientations

Thesis, and . . .

We are all different. For many of us, this is surprisingly hard to absorb: we may spend many years of our life in the deep, if unexamined, belief that everyone is in fact identical to us, and that if they appear otherwise it is because they are pretending, out of stubbornness or malice. Like the classic English person abroad, we believe that if we can only express ourselves loudly and repeatedly enough, everyone will understand our language. Letting go of this misperception, although hard, is also a blessed relief.

On the other hand, we are all much the same. Human beings seem to arrive on the planet with a very similar set of needs and faculties; we also go through a fairly stereotyped set of experiences. Interestingly, we seem to work hard to bring even quite unusual or bizarre experiences or congenital differences into line with the standard pattern. Among the many things we have in common, we all need to feel understood and to be accepted by other human beings.

The theory of character and personality types can illuminate both of these aspects of our humanity – our difference and our similarity. It can bind the two together into a paradoxical unity, where difference becomes similarity and similarity becomes difference. At its best, perhaps, it can offer a model for seeing how individual differences are an ordered set of ways in which we express our underlying similarity; and, equally, how we are all similar in the very fact of our individuality. More specifically, it can provide tools to help psychotherapists, psychologists and counsellors build bridges between their own sorts of difference, and those of their clients: tools for understanding and acceptance.

... Antithesis

On the other hand – or in the hands of other practitioners – personality typologies can become tools for alienation. They can, so it is claimed, justify a sort of therapy by numbers, a grossly oversimplified pseudo-system that shoehorns the client's reality into fixed pigeon-holes, supporting a false appearance of knowing on the part of the practitioner. The use of typologies can rob attention from the living, here-and-now relationship, and substitute a pathologized caricature for the unique flesh-and-blood individual who is the client. In another version of the paradox of difference and similarity, therapy should treat everyone exactly the same – that is, as unique, and therefore uniquely worthy of respectful study (Shlien 1989).

Synthesis

Which of these two accounts appeals is a matter of individual difference – or is, perhaps (we write somewhat tongue in cheek), an expression of the reader's personality type! As the old joke says, there are two kinds of people in the world: those who think there are two kinds of people in the world and those who don't. For some it is the dangers of typology that feel most important; while others would instead stress the benefits.

Perhaps it is possible to define some middle ground. It is surely unbelievable that someone could practise psychotherapy for 20 or 30 years and not think, when they meet a new client for the first time: 'Ah! I have come across this kind of person before', or 'This type of thinking reminds me of another client'. Psychotherapists and counsellors are, after all, specialists in people; and specialists develop categories, which are ways of sorting, storing and drawing upon the information they gather: information that has the potential to improve both their sensitivity and their understanding. Some 'people-categories' can reasonably be thought of as the distilled wisdom of our experience, both as individuals and as a group following a specialization that is at least a century old. Such wisdom is important to humanity; it is the reason why societies have usually honoured their old people, the reason why we record information and ideas, and the reason why burning books is generally equated with sacrilege.

At the same time, there is another type of wisdom that is increasingly being recognized in some quarters as having equal value, particularly in the measures of therapeutic effectiveness. This is the wisdom of 'beginner's mind' (Suzuki 1973), where wisdom consists in seeing everything as if for the first time, without the lens of learned assumptions or the filter of experience. The argument about the merits or dangers of character and personality types is, then, perhaps about the appropriate balance in psychotherapy and counselling between the wisdom of experience and the wisdom of 'beginner's mind'. And this balance – like all living balances – has to be a dynamic one, which sways between its two extreme positions in each session, and over a week, a year, a lifetime. For all practitioners, there may be times when the living flame of their work seems to be embodied in theories of character, and other times when truth resides in the abandonment of form in favour of raw content. We see these poles, for example, in Bion, who on the one hand produces his Grid (Bion 1963), which structures the process of thinking, but yet, on the other hand, urges the therapist to enter each session 'without memory or desire' (Bion 1970).

Within this context, and honouring both positions, we can examine in more detail the various arguments that can be made on both sides, for and against typologies – understanding them not as rigid alternatives, as either/or, but as different facets of truth between which we move in any period of time.

Effective practice

The core argument in favour of the use of typologies in psychotherapy must be that it facilitates effective practice. This can be argued on one of two bases, deriving respectively from what we may call 'realist' and 'post-modernist' positions. From a realist point of view, the argument is that the different personality types are clearly visible 'out there' in reality, constituting objective and dynamic distinctions between human beings. And that in acknowledging them, and understanding their different patterns and origins, we are bound to clarify and improve our therapeutic work.

The post-modernist position asserts the usefulness of typologies without concerning itself as to their objective truth. Systems, from this viewpoint, are created by human beings to facilitate their engagement with the world, rather than accurately to portray external reality. Systems reflect a whole range of cultural, historical, social and political positions (e.g. Gergen 1994). Character typology is thus a discourse (Foucault 1974) and should be evaluated as such, in terms of its power to articulate and to authorize aspects of therapeutic practice. The post-modernist supporter of typology, or of a particular typology, would argue that it helpfully privileges certain sorts of relationship between therapist and client (for example, the 'understanding and acceptance' to which we have already referred).

If character typologies are in fact objective, as the realist position asserts, then their usefulness is pretty much unarguable. Any valid systematic distinctions in psychological motivation and reaction patterns between different clients are bound to illuminate therapeutic work with those clients! What follows, however, is that by taking a realist position, we are also claiming that only one particular typology is valid (even if we do not yet know which one), and that all the others are erroneous. The post-modernist approach does not suffer from this problem: it can happily assert that any number of different typologies are equally valid, and proceed to assess them in terms of their flexibility, clarity, richness, political values and other such categories. To establish the basic usefulness of typologies as such, however, it may be claimed that we need to show that they facilitate therapeutic work by operational criteria – client satisfaction, improved functioning, non-return to therapy, and so on. No research of this kind has yet been done.

There is another way in which a post-modern view of typologies can argue for their value: it can be claimed that a rich and satisfying theory intrinsically benefits practice. If the therapist or counsellor feels nourished and supported in their work by a theoretical perspective that helps them have a sense of grasping the client's core issues, then surely this must be useful to their work – whether or not their feelings are objectively valid. There is a good deal of evidence that what is likely to make the experience of therapy effective is primarily the quality of relationship that develops between practitioner and client (e.g. Kazdin 1986). But what facilitates this relationship? Might not a satisfying and plausible typology increase practitioner confidence and thus improve the quality of the therapeutic relationship?

It is entirely possible, and indeed perhaps quite common, for someone to believe in both the 'realist' and the 'post-modernist' arguments that we have outlined. Despite the realist position that only one typology can in the end be correct, the contradictions are primarily at a philosophical level – and philosophical contradictions need not necessarily interfere with good practice.

Counter-arguments

The principal rejoinder to the realist argument for typologies must be as follows: typologies (or at least the preferred typology) are in fact not objective – the distinctions that the typology represent are not real, or not reliable, or lack predictive power. The equivalent counter-argument to the post-modernist version is: typologies in general (or certain typologies) are in fact not useful – the discourse of typologies is not a rich and fluent one; it does not facilitate the therapeutic relationship; it does not help.

Unfortunately, it is difficult to escape the post-modernist position, especially in the highly subjective field of psychotherapy and counselling. Objectivity has become a rather difficult and fragile concept: it is indeed generally recognized in many disciplines that all we ever have to work with is data, with descriptions of reality, rather than any immediately apprehensible reality itself. However, it still remains a meaningful and important question whether research data exist to support or to undermine different theories of character and personality type. The answer is not a simple one. Certainly there is evidence from psychology that there are meaningful and consistent patterns of personality traits, although there is considerable disagreement as to which are the best traits to pick out (Revelle 1995). There is also a degree of research support, at least in part, for several of the specific typologies which we will describe. We outline this at relevant points in the book. However, many of the typologies used in psychotherapy have been researched either insufficiently or not at all.

There is a further argument against the realist position that does not depend upon empirical research. It claims that typologies, by their nature, can only be extreme simplifications of human complexity; and that there are crucial elements in what constitutes each human being, which make that person essentially unique.

It must immediately be conceded that any typology is necessarily a simplification compared with the real, unique human being in front of us. This is the nature of typology in general: unless it is a schematized version of a complex reality, it could hardly add anything to our ability to grapple with that reality – a map has to be simpler than the territory it maps. Many typological systems acknowledge this by stressing that no individual is a pure example of one type: that people are mixtures of types, and the different proportions of different types create an individual character as unique as a fingerprint. (There are, nonetheless, ways of categorizing fingerprints to make for speedier identification.) The question is whether there is a meaningful relationship between the (relatively) simple schema and the actual human being: whether we can, at least theoretically, generate a complicated individual from the simple schema. This can only be resolved by looking at case studies, which try to do exactly that; and the judgement of their success is largely a subjective matter.

We also need to consider the argument that typologizing, independent of its truth status or otherwise, is not useful. Two main arguments are used in support of this position: that typologies tend to pathologize and that they deflect attention from what is actually happening in the here-and-now.

The argument about pathology applies in particular to approaches that derive from psychiatric and medically oriented systems (see the companion volume in this series on Psychopathology). These tend to emphasize deficit, dysfunction and deviation: they measure the actual individual against an imaginary norm, and define the ways in which he or she falls short. Indeed, 'he or she' is important, because some measures are extremely male-biased (see, for example, the study of sex role stereotypes in a group of mental health professionals in Broverman *et al.* 1970). The strongest criticism of such approaches comes from the humanistic schools of therapy, which are particularly hostile to the idea of therapy as a 'cure' for mental 'illness'. In recent years, however, the power of professionalization has propagated such ideas in many forms of therapy that would previously have angrily rejected them (see Chapter 5).

Like the 'simplification' claim, the 'here-and-now' argument applies to theoretical entities in general, not only to typologies. Basically, it suggests that what is crucial in psychotherapy is the quality of moment-by-moment relating, the intensity and accuracy of attention to every nuance of action and interaction; and that virtually any set of assumptions about what these actions and interactions signify, or what patterns they might fit into, is bound to blunt and deflect the therapist's ability to engage with the client's living reality. Bion's famous injunction to work 'without memory or desire' is matched by the anecdote that Carl Rogers would open the windows of his consulting room between sessions to refresh himself completely for the next person he was due to see.

From a very different point of view, the eminent post-Jungian therapist James Hillman argues that 'each life is formed by its unique image, an image that is the essence of our life and calls it to a destiny' (Hillman 1996: 39). On this basis he opposes not only the general therapeutic emphasis on the formative effects of childhood, parenting, trauma, and so on, but also the assimilation of the individual 'soul' to any sort of type or pattern. He thus redefines 'character' in a way much closer to its traditional, moral meaning than to its therapeutic use:

> Character forms a life regardless of how obscurely that life is lived and how little light falls on it from the stars.
> Calling becomes a calling to life . . . Calling to honesty rather than to success, to caring and mating, to service and struggle for the sake of living.
>
> (Hillman 1996: 255)

Perhaps it is a sufficient comment on such argument and anecdote – whether Bion, Rogers and Hillman – to repeat what we have already stated: that the use of typologies represents one polarity of a therapeutic spectrum, with the emphasis on individuality and the here-and-now as the opposite pole; and that these two forms of wisdom may both be necessary components of a whole therapy. Although therapeutic orientations differ in their enthusiasm or suspicion for typology, our own belief in the individual character of each therapist leads us to imagine that each practitioner will position herself or himself uniquely in what is for them the most comfortable and rewarding place in the continuum.

Classifying classifications

Having acknowledged and sketched out the arguments around typology, we can now focus on the different varieties of typology that have been developed and on how best to approach them.

Imagine that I want to sort out a tin of old buttons. How am I going to approach this task? I can work according to one or more of the more obvious distinguishing features – size, colour, texture. This will clearly be appropriate if I am thinking in terms of easily finding the right button for a particular mending job. If I am planning to use the buttons for an artistic or decorative purpose, rather than a practical one, I might use a different set of criteria, such as appearance. If I am working towards a history of button manufacture, I will be looking for more subtle features that provide me with clues as to the age of the buttons, their provenance, manufacturing process and of what material they are made. For specific purposes I might even want to classify them by the number of holes or by whether or not they have a rim around the edge. Along these lines, Frager (1994) classifies personality systems by how many fundamental types they describe, from two to twelve. The crucial point is that there is no single classification that we can define as right. Instead, we need to ask whether the classification we are using is appropriate for our purpose.

For therapists, the primary purpose of classifying people into groups is to facilitate effective treatment. Unfortunately, this simple formulation quickly decomposes into complexity once we look at it more closely. To begin with, there is the problematic question of what we mean by 'effective treatment'. In other words, what are the goals of therapy? Different schools and individuals have widely varying views on this, and the sort of character typologies they will favour vary correspondingly. The major distinction is between a goal of cure and correction and one of growth and insight. The first goal generates a discourse based on pathological entities, the second a discourse of preferred styles, of strengths and weaknesses.

Beyond this important issue, however, there are many other questions about 'effective treatment' that have an impact on character typology. For example, some therapeutic approaches stress the importance of a respectful sensitivity to the client's unique individuality and an approach of following rather than leading; such a therapy (e.g. person centred) may well avoid or de-emphasize typology. Other approaches are primarily outcome-focused, with a philosophy that it is what works that should be used; these (e.g. redecision therapy) favour typologies that offer a direct and simple relationship between classification and treatment (for both examples, see Chapter 5). Then there are approaches that stress the importance of a deep understanding of the client's early history. These tend to develop complex typologies that relate current styles to long-term life problems; examples include psychoanalysis (Chapter 2) and Reichian therapy (Chapter 3). Therapies that emphasize working in the 'here-and-now' may avoid typology altogether (Chapter 5), or they may use what they claim to be acausal, empirical systems – 'this is what we find' (e.g. Jungian analysis, Chapter 4). Therapies that seek to help clients connect with a transpersonal level of reality often use typologies; where they do so, the typology incorporates this aspect of experience (Chapter 6).

In the sections that follow, it is useful to keep one eye on how the different typologies relate to these questions of treatment strategy and therapeutic goals. We set out six different axes of 'button-sorting' methods:

- descriptive *vs* causal
- open *vs* closed
- tight *vs* fuzzy
- embodied *vs* mental
- pathological *vs* stylistic
- directive *vs* permissive

Most typologies are located somewhere along a spectrum between each of these polarized pairs. It is also important to remember that this is just one method of sorting, one which, in terms of our own categories, is descriptive, open, fuzzy, mental, stylistic and, hopefully, permissive.

Descriptive versus causal typologies

Perhaps the most fundamental difference among character typologies is between those which offer simply a taxonomy – a report on observed patterns – and those which claim to offer an explanation of those patterns, an account of how character types come into being. In Chapter 2 we describe the contrast between two such approaches within the field of psychoanalysis. Other examples of primarily descriptive systems are Jungian typology (Chapter 4), the Enneagram (Chapter 6) and DSM IV (see below). Examples of primarily causal systems are Reichian and post-Reichian character theory (Chapter 3), astrology (Chapter 6) and Ayurveda (also Chapter 6).

We should note at this point that the notion of causality – in general, not only in relation to personality – is a slippery and paradoxical one. Certainly a system's causal orientation says nothing about its plausibility or otherwise. A system could be based on the theory, say, that our character type is determined by the number plates on our parents' first car. Unless a mechanism to explain this relationship can be offered, the notion of causality is somewhat empty. More subtly, however, it can be argued that causal theories simply bump the issue further up the chain: one will always eventually arrive at a level where something 'just happens to happen' (e.g. the number plate on our parents' car was 'randomly generated' by the Vehicle Licensing Agency!). We return to this issue below.

A directly parallel dichotomy between causal and descriptive models exists in the field of the psychology of personality (Revelle 1995). The 'descriptivists' argue that causal explanations must be preceded by agreement on what there is to be explained. Working in a tradition that goes back to Plato and Galen, they look for ways of combining the multiplicity of behaviour traits into a small number of dimensional types. This process is not easy (Goldberg 1993), but there is wide agreement on five dimensions, which appear under various names but may be summed up as extraversion/introversion, agreeableness, conscientiousness, stability/neuroticism and openness to experience; a smaller number prefer the three dimensions of extraversion/introversion, emotional stability and psychoticism (Pervin 1990; Revelle 1995).

'Causalists', on the other hand, argue that many of the difficulties in achieving a workable taxonomy stem from the lack of underlying mechanisms to explain the various traits and their occurrence. They have mainly focused on biological explanations, involving differences in the activation of specific brain structures or in the relative amounts of specific neurotransmitters (Gale and Eysenck 1992), and tend to consider the three dimensions outlined above in terms of the biological concepts of approach and reward, inhibition and punishment, and aggression and flight (Eysenck 1991). Evolutionary theory has also been brought to bear on the issue (Buss 1991; Pinker 1998), although this approach has been forcefully questioned (Fodor 1998; Rose and Rose 2000).

Most people would agree that a causal typology is a more powerful model than a descriptive one – if it can be accepted as valid. It also makes sense to think that a causal model will be more therapeutically useful: understanding why someone is the way they are is likely – even if not certain – to provide pointers as to how this might be changed. Nevertheless, this is difficult to achieve within a psychology research paradigm; most of the causal explanations offered by schools of psychotherapy can neither be verified nor falsified, but depend on a judgement of intuitive plausibility or otherwise.

Open versus closed typologies

The crucial distinction here is between systems based on an ordering principle that defines the number and nature of types allowed, and more empirical systems that permit as many or as few types, and of whatever sort, as are actually observed. It is important to note that this axis is independent of the previous one; it is entirely possible for a typology to be descriptive and either open or closed, or closed and either descriptive or causal, and so on.

Closed systems, based on some superordinate organizing principle, can be interpreted as causal, in the special sense that the organizing principle itself is the logical cause of the types found, even though no causal mechanism is on offer. For example, astrology determines the basic number of types as twelve, no more and no less, since there are twelve signs of the zodiac, and so on with all of the variations and sub-types. Often these organizing principles derive from some source outside the realm of psychotherapy or psychology altogether. Systems like astrology or Tarot (Chapter 6) can be applied to psychotherapy, but are not intrinsically connected with that field; in fact, they cast an interesting light on the relationship between therapy and counselling on the one hand, and the traditional art of fortune-telling on the other. Number, in one way or another, is often the organizing principle for closed typologies; apart from astrology, the Jungian personality system (Chapter 4), like many others, is based on the number four, which Jung sees as an archetypal number of wholeness (von Franz 1974). The Enneagram system (Chapter 6) is based on the number nine and its mystical symbolism; Ayurvedic typology (Chapter 6) is organized around the number three, which also appears frequently in classical psychoanalysis – oral, anal, genital; id, ego, super-ego; mother, father, child (the oedipal triangle).

Such patterns exert a powerful magnetism on many theoreticians; the temptation to 'complete' a pattern for purely formal reasons is considerable. For example, in certain developments of Reichian character theory (Chapter 3), we find that a typological grid is constructed that moves away from Reich's original developmental structure towards what could be termed an aesthetically satisfying one (Southgate 1980; Boadella and Smith 1976). Perhaps there are parallels with the way in which mathematical physicists use aesthetic criteria to assess new theories, although the character theorists concerned might prefer the analogy of the Periodic Table, which was used to predict correctly the existence and characteristics of hitherto unknown elements through noting gaps in the formal pattern.

A good example of an open system, on the other hand, would be the structural version of psychoanalytic character theory (Chapter 2), which allows for the description of as many (or as few) character types as practitioners believe themselves to observe in their clinical work. Open systems have the strength of greater empiricism, with no formal issues to detract from direct observation; but also, perhaps, the weakness of that same empiricism, in that it offers no powerful theoretical tools for adjudicating between different observations.

Tight versus fuzzy typologies

The distinction between open and closed systems relates to some concepts from the field of category theory: the study of the conceptual processes involved in the organization of data into groups, types, etc. (Lakoff 1987). Category theory has had the important effect of allowing us freedom from the constraints of the classical Western understanding of categories, which turns out to misrepresent the ways in which categories are actually constructed and examples are assigned to them. Lakoff gives some examples of 'familiar ideas' that 'fall by the wayside'. These include: 'the mind is separate from, and independent of, the body'; 'reason is transcendental'; 'there is a correct, God's eye view of the world'; and 'all people think using the same conceptual system' (Lakoff 1987: 9).

Category theory is clearly of great potential significance; but for our immediate purposes, we can draw from it a valuable distinction between what we can call 'tight' and 'fuzzy' categories. To go back to our buttons, there are some ways of organizing them which set up groups that are watertight and 'either/or'; for example, a particular button either has two holes or it doesn't. Other categories, however, such as 'blue', are differently constructed. Some of our buttons will be thoroughly and unambiguously blue – excellent examples of the 'blue button' group. Others will be pale blue, dark blue, fairly blue, bluish, bluey-green, greenish-blue – until we reach a button that we tentatively identify as not blue but green.

Lakoff (1987: 56) puts this in more technical language as follows:

> Some categories, like tall man or red, are graded; that is, they have inherent degrees of membership, fuzzy boundaries, and central members whose degree of membership (on a scale from zero to one) is one ... Other categories, like bird, have clear boundaries; but within those boundaries ... some category members are better examples of the category than others.

A crucial point here is that 'fuzzy' categories are no less valid or definite than 'tight' ones. It is simply that many aspects of reality can be better treated through fuzzy categories than through tight ones.

Examples of fuzzy typologies include the Jungian system (Chapter 4; although this is often portrayed as tight, individuals are actually considered to be a mixture of traits: Jacobi 1968: 16–17) and Reichian character theory (Chapter 3). Tight typologies include sun-sign astrology (Chapter 6): each individual either is or is not a Leo, for example, even though their full chart combines the influence of many different signs. Lacanian psychoanalysis (Chapter 2) also uses a tight typology: any given individual is one, and only one, of the three categories neurotic, perverse or psychotic; and within the neurotic category is either obsessive or hysteric.

Embodied versus mental typologies

A different way of analysing the range of typologies distinguishes between systems that focus on body types, physiology, metabolism, neurochemistry and other such features, and those that in effect treat human beings as if they were disembodied mentalities. In a sense, many embodied typologies are necessarily 'causalist', suggesting as they do that the bodily or biological differences that they identify are the cause of psychological and behavioural differences. This form of causation, however, as we have suggested above, only pushes the problem back one step. Often a formulation such as 'this person's emotional disposition is caused by their neurochemistry' is only equivalent to 'this rose's redness is caused by the fact that it reflects light of a certain wavelength': it is just a re-statement of the premise in a different terminology. Our language for discussing 'minds' and 'bodies' is not yet sufficiently sophisticated to get us very far (Totton 1998).

Yet in addition to causalist embodied typologies there are also what we may call 'correlative' typologies. Again, astrology is a good example: there is wide agreement that certain body types correlate strongly with particular sun signs and/or ascendants, but both the physical and the psychological traits are seen as being determined in parallel by the astrological alignments. In line with the general assumptions of our culture, mental typologies would not normally be described as correlative, since personality is considered to be a primarily mental phenomenon. This assumption is perhaps worth questioning – we are, after all, embodied beings, who express ourselves through our embodiment. The 'mentalism' of our culture could itself be defined in terms of a particular character style within many of the systems we are considering (e.g. schizoid). As Jung argued strongly, our culture tends to privilege Thinking over Sensing, Feeling and Intuition. But Jung's own typology (Chapter 4) is unfortunately a good example of an essentially mental system!

However, Katherine Benziger's (1995, 1996) work 'embodies' Jung's 'mind' (see Chapter 4). Character as used in psychoanalysis (Chapter 2) is also understood mentally, even though its deep roots, like those of analysis in general, are in bodily experience (Totton 1998). Reichian character theory (Chapter 3) is a deeply embodied system; so is Sheldon's (1942) body typing (Chapter 5), which sees the body as explicitly the causal element. Ayurveda (Chapter 6) is another example of an embodied personality system.

Pathological versus stylistic typologies

Character typology in psychotherapy originated as a diagnostic tool. It assumed that the types to be identified were types of pathology; that is, different styles of mental illness. In fact, the first types to be used in psychotherapy were the psychiatric categories of Kraepelin (1917), the intellectual descendants of which survive to the present day in the pages of the fourth edition of the *Diagnostic and Statistical Manual* (DSM; American Psychiatric Association 1994).

This sort of typology is an example of what is known as 'nosology', the study and classification of disease. There are major philosophical and political issues involved in the definition of mental states or behaviours as forms of disease (see Banton *et al.* 1985, especially pp. 57–63; Penfold and Walker 1984). This emerges very clearly in the bitter struggle over the inclusion in earlier versions of the DSM of homosexuality as a mental illness, something which was changed only in the 1980 edition, with declassification by the World Health Organization being as late as 1992. Pett (2000: 55) claims this was the result of the development of humanistic approaches to therapy. The general issues here are not our concern, however – only the leaking into psychotherapy of the notion of character as a pathological entity, a sort of watered-down version of a psychiatric condition. For example, the 'schizoid' character might be seen as diluted schizophrenia, or the 'hysteric' character as diluted hysteria.

In the typologies we describe, three main positions emerge on all this: (1) character is pathological; (2) character is value-neutral; and (3) character can manifest in either balanced or extreme forms. All three of these points of view are argued within psychoanalysis (Chapter 2) and within Reichian and post-Reichian therapy (Chapter 3). Jungian work tends to take the second position, while examples of the third viewpoint are Transactional Analysis and Sheldon's (1942) somatotyping (both Chapter 5).

Directive versus permissive typologies

Somewhat related to the previous axis is the sixth, between typologies that have built into them a specification of how each type should or needs to change, so as more closely to approximate to perfect health, and typologies that are more concerned to approach each type and each individual with interest and sympathy, supporting them in their particular quest, and using an understanding of type as a helpful tool in this permissive process. The directive approach has a strong relationship with the medical or engineering model of psychotherapy, the idea that clients (or patients) are coming to the practitioner to get 'fixed'; while the permissive approach is linked with the 'personal growth movement' and person centred approaches to therapy, which try to focus on the client's goals rather than those of the practitioner.

Explicit examples of the first type include Ayurveda and the Enneagram (Chapter 6) and Gestalt interruption theory (Chapter 5); this is also the underlying assumption of much analytic and Reichian work (Chapters 2 and 3). Other Reichians and analysts take the opposite viewpoint, as do systems including astrology (Chapter 6), Jungian analysis (Chapter 4) and Transactional Analysis (Chapter 5), although some observers claim that many of these therapies actually smuggle in prescriptive notions.

What makes an effective typology?

In working through the next five chapters, readers will doubtless look for ways to evaluate and choose between the systems we describe. We imagine that each person will do this from their own value basis, and we have no intention of substituting one of our own. However, we hope that the descriptive axes outlined above may be helpful in evaluating the many typologies we describe. It may also be of assistance in offering some suggestions as to what qualities might be expected of a good typology. These are obviously open to argument, but arguing with them may also help readers define their own ideas. Whether any existing typology achieves these standards is an interesting question.

We believe that for a typology to be effective, it should be powerful. By this, we mean that it should do some work – it should offer strong distinctions, ways of cutting through the data to reveal underlying patterns. It should not simply move the material around into new patterns on the same level of description. It should not leave a large remainder of superfluous data which do not fit within the schema; nor should there be large degrees of uncertainty as to what fits where.

It should also be coherent. Its categories should bear clear relationship to each other, should form some sort of rational whole, should be expressed in a clear and consistent vocabulary, and should be visibly on the same level of explanation and description as each other.

It should have an explanatory function. Once material has been processed by the system, it should make more sense, have more pattern to it and, ideally, be related to patterns of causation that are prior in time or logical sequence.

An effective typology should be predictive: we should be able to deduce, from where a person fits into the system, that they are likely to act, think and feel in certain ways. It should also be productive of treatment strategies: we should be able to deduce from it that certain techniques, modes of communication, and so on will be more useful with this client than other ones.

To all this, perhaps we should add a simple but crucial point made by Jung: that a typology of personality should help people – practitioners and clients alike – to understand and accept each other as they are.

CHAPTER 2

Character in psychoanalysis

> Observation teaches us that individual human beings realize
> the general picture of humanity in an almost infinite variety
> of ways. If we yield to the legitimate need to distinguish par-
> ticular types in this multiplicity, we shall, at the start, have the
> choice as to what characteristics and what points of view we
> shall take as the basis of our differentiation. For that purpose
> physical qualities will doubtless serve no less well than mental
> ones; the most valuable distinctions will be those which prom-
> ise to present a regular combination of physical and mental
> characteristics.
>
> (Freud 1931: 361)

The concept of character has been part of psychoanalytic thinking
from very early on, ever since Freud's paper 'Character and anal
eroticism' pointed out that 'we often come across a type of person
who is marked by a particular set of character traits, while at the
same time our attention is drawn to the behaviour in his childhood
of one of his bodily functions and the organ concerned in it' (Freud
1908: 209). This formulation launches one of the three major approaches to character recognized in psychoanalysis; unfortunately,
however, these three systems – the *descriptive*, the *structural* and the
dynamic – although in many ways incompatible and antagonistic, are
not clearly distinguished by most analysts (Baudry 1984). The story
of the use of character theory in psychoanalysis and psychodynamic
therapy is a complex and tangled one, illustrating many of the general
themes and issues that we have already highlighted, in particular
the question of whether or not character is a pathological entity.

Character and symptom

Central to psychoanalytic thinking in this area is the polarity between *character* and *symptom*. On the one hand, a symptom is any piece of behaviour or experience that individuals regard as strange, unpleasant and alien to themselves. Some examples are phobias, obsessions and psychosomatic illnesses. In contrast, there are other aspects of behaviour or experience which, while they may seem to others equally idiosyncratic and perhaps undesirable, are completely acceptable to a person, who may say things like 'But that's just who I am'. This second group makes up an assemblage which psychoanalysis refers to as character (Gitelson [1954] 1989; Baudry 1989).

This simple and neat opposition has been subjected to considerable modification. Reich (1972: 45), for example, argues cogently that 'the symptom-neurosis is always rooted in a neurotic character', so that, as Issacharoff (1991: 720) puts it, 'every analysis must be a character analysis'. In other words, character is the root system from which symptoms sprout. However, it is still generally agreed that, while 'there is no person without a character' (Stein 1969: 465) – in other words, every human being has a more or less fixed set of behavioural and emotional predispositions – each person may or may not experience symptoms at a particular moment in time. The distinction between symptom and character, with its implication that character consists of patterns of reaction that have been deeply worked into the fabric of our self-identification, is still a very helpful one. It illuminates, among other things, why character changes far less readily than do symptom patterns.

The descriptive approach

Psychoanalysts frequently employ what in Chapter 1 we called a *descriptive* approach to character. In doing this they tend to take over wholesale the psychiatric categories of psychopathology, applying them not only to those seen as mentally ill, but also to comparatively normal individuals whose characterological make-up is understood to have within it the potential for a particular pathology. As a rough analogy, 'the London road' *ends* in London, but it can *begin* anywhere. So a 'phobic character' may not actually experience phobias as such; but under appropriate conditions of stress, they are likely to develop phobias rather than any other symptom.

Alternatively, under similar conditions, an 'obsessive character' might develop an obsessive-compulsive disorder, and so on. Bergmann (1980) describes one particular 'phobic character' whose frigidity in his example was interpreted as concealing a fear of the penis. Her character structure is understood to be a type of binding and masking of earlier explicit phobias into a generalized fearfulness rooted in a 'confusion about real and imaginary dangers' (p. 543), which Bergmann derives from the patient's mother. Clearly, the concept of 'appropriate conditions of stress' begs several questions about causality; and how is one to test whether someone is a 'phobic character' unless they develop phobias?

This descriptive system of character operates on two levels: one of specific pathologies, as in the examples above, and one of general type. On this second level, analysts distinguish between and describe the 'neurotic character' (Glover 1926; Alexander 1930), the 'psychotic character' (Frosch 1964) and the 'perverse character' (Chasseguet-Smirgel 1974), corresponding to the central tripartite diagnostic categories of psychoanalysis. On a more specific level, the types of character identified include, besides the 'phobic' and the 'obsessional', the 'hysterical' (Easser and Lesser 1965), the 'narcissistic' (Bursten 1973), the 'masochistic' (Brenner 1959) and the 'schizoid' (Khan 1966; Guntrip 1968), as well as others. A further diagnostic category is 'character disorder', sometimes equated with the borderline personality, 'generally applied to chronic maladaptive patterns, inflexible in nature and generally experienced as ego-syntonic' (Baudry 1984: 466).

The tripartite division into neurotic, psychotic and perverse characters tends to be accounted for dynamically, structurally or both; but everything we said in Chapter 1 about the limitations of descriptive character systems applies to the specific level, which is essentially just a way of organizing data, inherited from Kraepelinian psychiatry. In itself it implies no theory of the origins or development of character structure, except that it biases its users towards a pathological conception of character. As with any nosological system, it is easy to lose sight of the fact that *only* a theory of origins can establish whether meaningful, non-factitious entities are being discussed; and easy therefore to end up asking questions like 'What gives rise to the phobic character?' rather than the more appropriate question 'What do we agree to mean by the term "phobic character", and is this term a useful one?' This is evident in the Bergmann (1980) article cited above, where the explanatory argument is clearly *ex post facto*.

Several authors have made this point and have argued that the descriptive system is not in itself psychoanalytic (Stein 1969: 466; Baudry 1989: 467). As Baudry (1984) suggests, the specifically psychoanalytic conception of character has a double focus, combining 'first the clinical observation of certain traits as a stable cluster, second the establishment of a relation between a superficial piece of behavior and a deep structure' (p. 456). A phobic attitude, to stay with the same example, is in this sense superficial; and since character refers to a deep structure, a concept such as 'phobic character' conflates different levels. Often, therefore, the descriptive system is supplemented or underpinned with one or both of the two theories of character described below, despite the difficulties involved in conflating any of these theories.

The dynamic approach

The original psychoanalytic approach to character, which we will call the *dynamic* interpretation, matches Baudry's description: it relates behavioural traits to the 'deep structure' of the *drives*. Drives (inaccurately translated in the *Standard Edition* of Freud's work as the 'instincts'; see Ornston 1992: 93–5) are a central concept of Freud's original work, played down in later ego-focused developments of psychoanalysis. The term refers to a pressure, originally organismic but taking on psychological qualities, which impels us towards an object (frequently another person) to relieve the state of tension that the drive induces in us (Laplanche and Pontalis 1988: 214–17). Freud changed his mind at various points about exactly which drives operate in human beings, but sexuality – in its broad psychoanalytic sense of the urge to sensual satisfaction or 'libido' – is always central to his picture.

The dynamic interpretation of character considers what happens to the drives as an individual passes through the stages of developmental experience between birth and about 5 years of age. During this period, the theory holds, our libidinal energy focuses in turn on different 'erogenous zones': the mouth, the anus, the penis or clitoris, and the whole genital region. Hence, the developmental stages are referred to as the oral, the anal, the phallic and the genital stages. In the 1908 paper referred to above, Freud makes a bold hypothesis about what he refers to as the *anal* character. He suggests that we can regularly observe people who combine the three traits of *orderliness*, *parsimony* and *obstinacy*, and that this combination of adult traits derives from a childhood struggle to overcome a particular pleasure in anal activity.

These traits are what Freud terms a 'reaction-formation': unconsciously, he argues, the individual concerned wants to be messy, splurging and yielding, as an expression of anal eroticism. As a defence against and a denial of these unacceptable feelings, the person in effect 'constipates' their mode of expression in ways which (like the classic description of a symptom; Laplanche and Pontalis 1988: 376–8) combine the satisfaction of an impulse with its simultaneous denial and concealment. However, unlike a symptom, the characterological pattern is integrated deeply into the individual's sense of self; we do not generally experience our own character as a problem.

Freud's hypothesis about the anal character was taken up enthusiastically by other analysts, notably Jones ([1918] 1977) and Abraham (1923, 1925, 1926), the latter's writing in particular describing the three major characters – oral, anal and genital. In this way, there developed a general theory of character linked to the simultaneous expression and denial of libidinal issues relating to each developmental phase. Thus, while the anal character demonstrates orderliness, parsimony and obstinacy – or, in some cases, the opposites of these three traits – the oral character tends to be dominated by neediness (or self-sufficiency), appetite (or asceticism) and volubility (or incommunicativeness); and so it is similarly with the other characters. In other words, life themes and activities connected to the relevant erogenous zone and developmental stage are highlighted or exaggerated in one way or another. Because character can be defined as much by absence of certain traits as by their presence, to some extent the descriptions are rendered less convincing by their implicit use of a 'heads I win, tails you lose' argument, which means that nothing can escape categorization. However, the essential issue is the increased focus on particular areas of life.

Otto Fenichel (1941: 174–5) introduced a very helpful way of seeing the two opposing forms in which each character appears. He distinguished broadly between the *sublimation* type and the *reactive* type of character structure – that is, between a character who tries to *express* unconscious desire in indirect and socially acceptable forms, and a character who takes a different tack and tries to *deny* that desire. Thus, to take a simple example, an oral desire to suckle might give rise to a sublimatory character where the person becomes a connoisseur of food and drink, and also finds subtle ways to attract other people's support and nurturing; or it might give rise to a reactive ('compensated oral') character, an ascetic lone wolf who denies any need for contact with others and treats eating and drinking purely as a practical necessity.

Table 2.1 summarizes the basic, traditional psychoanalytic view of character structure, as it relates to the child's development through oral, anal, phallic and genital stages of fixation. It should be noted that probably no one writer would agree with every detail in the table, and that there are innumerable further complexities and subtleties in the psychoanalytic literature on character.

This dynamic theory was given powerfully coherent expression by Wilhelm Reich, during the period when he was still a respected and significant member of the International Psychoanalytic Association (Reich 1972). Reich's special interest during this time was in developing a systematic approach to clinical technique, a subject that had previously received little attention. His conclusion was that clinical effectiveness depended on tackling the analysand's *resistance*, and that the foundation of this resistance, the epitome of psychic resistance in general, was the character structure. According to this understanding, character becomes not just an interesting piece of theory, but a key element of practice.

Reich (1972: 155) defined character as '*an armouring of the ego* against the dangers of the outside world and the repressed drive demands of the id' (original emphasis). This armouring is encountered in therapy as a *style of defence*, as the form, rather than the content, of what the analysand produces: for example, an air of vagueness, or intensity, or superiority, or appeasement, would each represent a particular characterological defence, irrespective of the specific material. In daily life, this armouring defends the individual in complex ways against unacceptable desires. In therapy, it is used to defend *against the analyst*, to stop the therapist uncovering those desires. Reich thus emphasized the polarity already described between the specific symptom, which is frequently the identified 'problem' of the analysis, and the much more diffuse and elusive character structure which gives form to the analysand's resistance. However:

> The character resistance which is manifested in terms of form is just as capable of being resolved with respect to its content, and of being traced back to infantile experiences and drive interests as the neurotic symptom is.
>
> (Reich 1972: 52)

Interestingly, Reich's view of character identifies him as an early object relations theorist. Character, he argued, originates in our fundamental experiences of relationship:

Table 2.1

	Age	Developmental traits	Sublimatory traits	Reactive traits
Oral	Birth to 2 years	Libido focused on the mouth and the activity of feeding. Issues of nurturing and dependency. Can be divided into 'sucking' and 'biting' phases *Metaphor*: eating/being eaten	Focus on appetite, on getting needs met by others. May be hearty and energetic; or needy, demanding and bitter	Denial of need or dependency. Presents appearance of self-sufficiency and competence. Often cares for others
Anal	2–4 years	Libido focused on anus. Toilet-training leads to issues of self-control, self disgust, rage and destructiveness *Metaphor*: expulsion/retention	Messy and chaotic, often aggressively so. Often drawn to money and/or working with hands. May show masochistic or sadistic (crushing) traits	'Orderliness, parsimony and obstinacy'. Disciplined and hard-working, but uncreative. Rigid and formal with a lack of spontaneity
Phallic	4–6 years	Libido focused on penis/clitoris (not yet distinguished by child). Culmination of Oedipus complex *Metaphor*: castration threat	Competitive, forceful and assertive, with a fear of collapse and yielding. Conventionally masculine. May show sadistic (piercing) traits	Self-controlled, sober and mild-mannered. Often highly moralistic about self and others. Can be persecuting
Hysteric	4–6 years	Corresponds to a failure fully to achieve the genital stage of development. Libido focused in the penis and vagina respectively, but with great anxiety *Metaphor*: seduction	Highly sexualized, provocative style, but actual sex may provoke panic and flight. Conventionally feminine, often with some transgressive traits	Asexual presentation, often with stiff, child-like appearance (which may itself be attractive). Difficulty with gender roles

On an elementary level, there is but one desire which issues from the biopsychic unity of the person, namely the desire to discharge inner tensions . . . This is impossible without contact with the outer world. Hence, the *first* impulse of *every* creature must be the desire to establish contact with the outer world.

(Reich 1972: 271, original emphasis)

Our experience of frustrated contact gives form to a character structure that both conceals and promotes, expresses and protects, our desire. The form taken depends upon the libidinal phase at which traumatic frustration is experienced (Reich 1972: 175). 'A person's character conserves and at the same time wards off the function of certain childhood situations' (Reich 1973: 305). And as we shall see in Chapter 3, Reich showed how character is directly expressed in the structure of an individual's *body*, via the pattern of muscular tensions which embodies their resistances.

The dynamic system of character, especially as developed by Reich and subsequent therapists, brings together three parameters: the *historical* (developmental), the *attitudinal* and the *bodily*. It achieves just what Freud asks for in the quotation which begins this chapter: 'a regular combination of physical and mental characteristics' – firmly anchored in a detailed account of how each individual character structure originates in situations of childhood repression and deprivation. The dynamic theory has also received a degree of support from research evidence. From a survey of research, Fisher and Greenberg (1977: 80–169) suggested that both the familiar anal traits of orderliness, parsimony and obstinacy, and oral characteristics like dependency, pessimism and passivity, do in fact frequently cluster together. 'We are impressed,' they concluded, 'with Freud's underlying idea that it is meaningful to analyze personality traits in the context of how they are related to body zones' (Fisher and Greenberg 1977: 165). However, there is less support for the relationship between character and developmental issues – and, interestingly, little research of any kind on the phallic character structure! (cf. Kline 1972: 44, 93–4).

Nonetheless, despite its combination of empirical support and internal coherence, the dynamic theory of character has been generally neglected within psychoanalysis since the 1930s, partly because of the dominance of ego-psychological approaches, but perhaps more specifically because of the expulsion of Reich (for reasons not directly connected with his views on character; see Sharaf 1983: 186–91). His work therefore continued entirely outside psychoanalytic circles. We look at this development in Chapter 3.

The structural approach

The dominant version of character which has been developed within the analytic world can be described as the *structural* interpretation. It grows mainly out of the 'ego psychology' developed by Anna Freud (1936) on the basis of her father's later theories. Character according to this approach has been succinctly defined by Fenichel (1945: 467) as consisting of 'the ego's habitual modes of adjustment to the external world, the id, and the superego'. In other words, it describes the particular style in which a given individual attempts to maintain a viable compromise between the demands of desire (id), morality (superego) and reality (external world). As Anna Freud (1936: 284) put it, character is 'approximately the whole set of attitudes habitually adopted by an individual ego for the solution of the never-ending series of inner conflicts'.

Here in a nutshell is the difference between the structural and the dynamic theories: while the latter is centred on *conflict*, the former is centred on *compromise*. One could say that the dynamic theory in a sense sides with the id, and describes its direct and indirect efforts to achieve its libidinal goals, whereas the structural theory sides with the ego as the site of compromise within the psyche, and as the agency which has the task of achieving that compromise. The sort of *status quo* described by the dynamic theory, although it represents a balance of opposing forces, is quite unlike a compromise: it is a paradoxical and tense synthesis in which both 'sides' express themselves fully through the same behaviours and attitudes, rather than agreeing on something part way between the two. The structural approach assumes that there is nothing innately conflictual in our psychic structure, but rather a 'hardwired' tendency to accommodation and adjustment between the different agencies, centred on the ego as privileged participant.

If we look at the structural interpretation of character in terms of the criteria established in Chapter 1, we see that, although it offers more of an explanatory narrative than the descriptive interpretation, it still contains arbitrary elements. It tends to ascribe the specific choice of character style to a vague summation of competing forces. There is no clear thread of meaning to knit together the range of ways in which a character expresses itself. Although there is a relatively powerful system for differentiating the character types in terms of the different balance of power between id, superego and external forces, the structural system lacks an account of *why* this balance differs from person to person.

Freud himself later shifted from the dynamic to the structural approach, 'execut[ing] a sweeping change in emphasis – from character as derivative of libidinal drives to character as derivative of identifications with the parents in the form of structured ego representations' (Liebert 1989: 50). This was, of course, only part of a general 'sweeping change of emphasis' whereby Freud's attention moved from the id and the drives to the ego and its construction out of processes of internalization and projection (Freud 1923); it is a controversial question whether, in his later work, Freud actually *rejected* his earlier positions or simply moved on to different investigations. In any case, Freud's shift does not represent a specific judgement on the merits of the different character theories, but relates to general issues in analytic metapsychology. Blos observes that Freud's later writing (Freud 1939) suggests that 'it is the fate of object libido that determines the character (e.g. the narcissistic or anaclitic character)' (Blos 1968: 246). A narcissistic character is one who is preoccupied with himself or herself; an anaclitic character someone who is concerned for relationships with others, or in anaclitic disturbances is pre-occupied with the state of relationships with others. Bursten (1973: 288), however, asserted that, in proposing these terms, Freud was not describing character types, citing:

> We have not, however, concluded that human beings are divided into two sharply differentiated groups, according as their object choice conforms to the anaclitic or the narcissistic type; we assume rather that both types of object choice are open to each individual, though he may show a preference for one or the other.
>
> (Freud 1914: 88)

During the 1930s, there was an explicit battle between the dynamic and structural views of character, as represented by Wilhelm Reich and by Anna Freud respectively. In *The Ego and the Mechanisms of Defence*, Anna Freud (1936: 33) criticizes what she sees as Reich's view of character:

> Since [characterological] modes of defence have become permanent, we cannot now bring their emergence and disappearance into relation with the emergence and disappearance of instinctual demands and affects from within ... Hence their analysis is a peculiarly laborious process. I am sure that we are justified in placing them in the foreground only when we can

detect no trace at all of a present conflict between ego, instincts and affect. And I am equally sure that there is no justification for restricting the term 'analysis of resistance' to the analysis of these particular phenomena, for it should apply to that of all resistances.

Thus, from the structural viewpoint, character becomes less crucial in terms of clinical technique. Nevertheless, it is still a highly important concept, and one which produces a continuing stream of papers and monographs refining the picture of each identified type and campaigning for the recognition of new types. A further difference between the structural and dynamic approaches is that for the former, unlike the latter, there is no *a priori* limit to the number of character types one can distinguish: in our terminology, it is an open system.

Later innovations

The concept of character is more or less universal within psychoanalysis; however, each analytic school redefines and re-describes character in its own preferred terminology and context. It is not clear that these later descriptions necessarily add very much to the collective understanding. Nevertheless, the major innovations in character theory are as follows.

Erikson

As part of his concerted effort to make analytic thinking more generally available, Erik Erikson (1959) re-launches the concept of character as 'identity', which he defines as 'both a persistent sameness within oneself and a persistent sharing of some kind of character with others' (p. 109). Striving to achieve identity becomes a central value in his scheme of human nature. As the quotation indicates, identity is not solely an individual matter, but also an expression of group attitudes. Erikson maps out a series of psycho-social crises through which identity 'emerges as an *evolving configuration* ... gradually established by successive ego syntheses and resyntheses throughout childhood' (p. 125). His picture of these crises largely conforms with that of ego psychology, but with the innovation that he extends the concept of developmental phases from early childhood (oral, anal and phallic/genital) and into adolescence to encompass the whole life of the individual, proposing eight 'ages' in all. In doing so, he largely abandons two crucial elements of psychoanalysis: sexuality and infancy. His account of development no longer places special emphasis on the events of early childhood, and it re-interprets the Freudian developmental stages in a way which de-emphasizes libidinal pleasure. Thus, for example, his description of the oral phase shifts the emphasis from breast-feeding and weaning to speech as a psycho-social accomplishment, and from the issue of oral libido to that of trust.

The significance of relationships – to parents and others – in psychosocial development situates Erikson somewhere between ego psychology and object relations. Yet Erikson (1965) also accords an important place to the natural environment in character development on a cultural scale, for instance drawing parallels between the generosity of the Sioux Indians (p. 123) and the former wealth of natural resources in the Prairies; and equally between the anal retentiveness in the life of the Yurok people and their need to preserve the cleanliness of the river so as to live on the limited stocks of salmon (p. 162). Implied in this are interesting questions of tribal, racial or national character, which Erikson (1965) raises in Part Four of *Childhood and Society*. Indeed, Erikson represents what Blos (1968: 246) calls the 'fourth approach' to classical psychoanalytic characterology: 'the influence of environment, culture, and history that engraves a patterned and preferential style of life on people (the psychosocial definition of character)'.

Fromm

Fromm, like Erikson, emigrated to the United States in the 1930s, and was similarly aware of the implications of life in different cultures for the development of personality. As Grey (1992: 345) writes:

> Fromm demonstrated . . . that socio-economic institutions and conditions mold our personalities, and that our personalities, in turn, guide our destinies. Fromm would see this restatement of Freud's well-known dictum about anatomy as more rhetorical than complete. Destiny is the outcome of multiple influences – biological, societal – and how the complexity of phenomena designated by these abstractions interacts with still other events.

Like Erikson, Fromm tends to de-emphasize sexuality in his 'humanized' account of psychoanalysis. Therefore, although he very much highlights a conception of character in ways that are sometimes close to Reich's views, he tries to substitute a generalized Eros for libido as the driving force (Fromm 1973: 59–60); thus he can portray the anal character, for example, not as an erotic response to repression but simply as 'one form of relatedness to others' (Fromm 1960: 249–50). There is something constructive, as we shall see in the next chapter, about this broadening out of the concept of character; but Fromm casts psychoanalytic character adrift from the body and substitutes no alternative causal dynamic. He rechristens analytic character structures in various different ways at different times; for example, in *Man For Himself* (Fromm 1947), he speaks of the 'receptive' character (equivalent to oral-dependent), the 'exploitative' (oral-sadistic), the 'hoarding' (anal) and the 'marketing' (phallic).

Object relations

The object relations school of psychoanalysis thinks of character – as it thinks of most psychological entities – as a function of the early relationship between infant and mother. In the British object relations tradition, the stress has been on the 'basic fault' (Balint 1968), the fundamental sense of lack within the self that arises from problematic mothering and gives rise to a split between 'true self' and 'false self' (Winnicott 1960). It is difficult to find much reference to character types, for example, in Melanie Klein, although Hinshelwood (1997) refers to a set of notes in the archives in the Wellcome Library ('Notes about character formation and inner relationships with reference to castration complex') that 'dwell on ideas about character which are more explicit than in any of her published work' (p. 885). He suggests that they are reminiscent of contemporary Kleinian understanding of the severe borderline character (Joseph 1989; Steiner 1993). Klein was more interested in 'positions' – the paranoid-schizoid and depressive positions – which contribute greatly to the formation of personality, but have a fluidity that makes them far less structured than any notion of character type.

The British school has not generally been given to systematic taxonomies. Development of the implications of these ideas in terms of specific character structures has been in the hands of the American school, most particularly Otto Kernberg (1989a,b), whose attempt to synthesize the three versions of character is treated below.

Self psychology

For Heinz Kohut's (1971, 1977) self psychology, character – again, like everything else – is a matter not of conflict or compromise, but of *deficit*. As with the object relations school, he links characterological problems with difficulties in the infant–mother relationship: specifically, with a failure of empathy on the mother's part leading to a failure of healthy narcissistic development, and the development of a 'borderline character'. This has a distinct resemblance to the 'basic fault' of Balint.

Lacan

Lacanian psychoanalysis applies very strongly the traditional division of human beings into neurotic, perverse and psychotic; it does not allow the possibility of the 'normal' or 'healthy' alternative to these three categories, which other analysts often (and rather vaguely) speak of. Within the neurotic group, there is a bipolar distinction between the hysteric and the obsessive, which can in some ways be compared to a characterology.

The hysteric position, in Lacanian thinking, is also understood as the position of the woman, and the obsessive position as that of the man (Fink 1995: 106–8). This does not relate to biological gender, but to one's unconscious identification, based on two different relationships to the phallus and, therefore, two different relations to language and to sexual desire. Such a short summary does little justice to the complexity of Lacanian ideas, but illustrates the possibility of exploring character further in his work.

Synthesis

Unsurprisingly, many attempts have been made to synthesize the different approaches to character which we have outlined. Often these attempts have ignored very real differences and contradictions, proceeding as if the approaches can simply be conflated. Thus Stein (1969: 462) presents a single grand list of all the different ways in which character has been conceived:

The breadth of character is enormous, as the whole of an individual's stable functioning is included under its heading. Character traits . . . represent an amalgam – a synthesis that expresses under one heading a combination including derivatives of drive, defence, identifications, superego aspects . . . The libidinal level has to be considered the prime factor; a close second would be the major mechanisms of defence; a third would be the nature of the person's object relations; next would follow the major fashions in which the person's self-esteem is regulated; other elements would include description of the person's major identifications and an assessment of the person's moral code and values . . .

Efforts such as this are perhaps more confusing than helpful; character becomes a bulging portmanteau, which, as Stein (1969: 463) acknowledges, 'falls just a bit short of a complete metapsychological profile'. Less even-handedly, other theorists try to show that everyone else's formulations can be subsumed within their own. Most notably, Kernberg (1989a: 191) offers to 'clarify the relationship between a descriptive structural diagnosis' – that is, a psychiatric descriptive pathology – 'and a metapsychological, especially structural, diagnosis'. He does so by superimposing his own version of the structural approach onto the dynamic approach, and then assuming that a preponderance of dynamic issues – 'instinctually infiltrated' character traits – indicates a severe pathology. Kernberg (1989b: 211) argues that 'unconscious intrapsychic conflicts are not simply conflicts between impulse and defense, but are between two opposing sets or units of internalized object relations. Both impulse and defense find expression through an affectively imbued internalized object relation'. On this basis, he takes up and re-interprets Fenichel's classification of character types (see p. 21).

Kernberg (1989a) takes over Fenichel's distinction between sublimatory and reactive character traits, but sets up a hierarchy with sublimatory traits at the top ('normal' character), followed by reactive traits ('higher' pathological character), reactive mixed with instinctual expression ('intermediate' pathological character) and instinctually infiltrated character defences ('lower' pathology). He correlates this entire system with the quality of internalized object relationships displayed by each 'level'. This is not so much a genuine synthesis, more a take-over bid – the most sophisticated of several such bids mounted from within different analytic schools. Table 2.2 summarizes Kernberg's system.

Table 2.2

Level of organization	Structure	Main defence	Object relations	Libidinal development	Example
Higher	Well-integrated but strict super-ego; stable ego	Repression; mainly inhibitory or phobic, with some reaction formations	Deep and stable; capable of guilt, mourning, etc.	Oedipal/genital	Hysterical; obsessive-compulsive; depressive-masochistic
Intermediate	Less integrated, stricter super-ego; primitive ego-ideal; ego under pressure	Repression, with some dissociation, projection and denial; more reaction, less inhibition	Fairly stable, able to form lasting involvements and to tolerate ambivalence and conflict	Regression to pre-genital conflicts, especially oral, although genital level has been attained	Oral; passive-aggressive; sado-masochistic; hysteroid; perverse
Lower	Minimal super-ego integration, with persecutory projections; split and fragmented ego	Projection and projective identification; dissociation	Weak, with impaired capacity for guilt and self-criticism	Pre-genital, sado-masochistic needs predominate	Infantile narcissistic; socio-pathic; impulsive; pre-psychotic; extreme perversions

Character – normal or abnormal?

In a brilliant paper, Ernest Jones (1918) was the first to point out that both attractive and unattractive qualities derive from the expression of, for example, the anal character. Among the negative anal character traits he lists:

> the incapacity for happiness, the irritability and bad temper, the hypochondria, the miserliness, meanness and pettiness, the slow-mindedness and proneness to bore, the bent for dictating and tyrannising, and the obstinacy.
>
> (Jones [1918] 1977: 437)

But among the positive:

> may be reckoned especially the individualism, the determination and persistence, the love of order and power of organization, the competency, reliability and thoroughness, the generosity, the bent towards art and good taste, the capacity for unusual tenderness, and the general ability to deal with concrete objects of the material world.
>
> (Jones [1918] 1977: 436–7)

We can observe immediately that while 'generosity' appears in the positive list, 'meanness' features in the negative: an accurate reflection of the way in which a given character position will manifest as either 'a' or 'anti-a', either a particular trait or, by negation, its opposite. This relates to Fenichel's later distinction between 'reactive' and 'sublimatory' character traits. In this example, it is the 'sublimatory' trait – meanness, disguising anal retentiveness – which is seen as negative, and the 'reactive' trait – generosity – as positive. (Although generosity may also sublimate the use of faeces as gifts – the distinction between reaction and sublimation is not simple.) But, for example, the 'sublimatory' traits of 'determination and persistence, the love of order', and so on all appear in the positive list.

Jones understands that anal traits, like all character traits, provide a necessary part of a rounded human personality. This understanding is the basis of the general psychoanalytic position that 'character is an aspect of the individual's functioning which implies neither health nor pathology. There is no person without a character' (Stein 1969: 465). However, there are large differences of emphasis around this issue, which tend to polarize around the Anna Freud/Wilhelm

Reich battle in the 1930s. The Anna Freudian structuralists have a basically normative version of human development and functioning, implicitly founded upon a picture of society as basically benevolent; while Reich and those aligned with him see society as in many ways a damaging force, which imposes character structures that are in practice pathological (Totton 2000: 62–4).

We look at Reich's views on this in the next chapter. Perhaps the most explicit proponent of the Anna Freudian position is Erikson, who offers a powerful re-reading of the Freudian/Reichian character model in terms of social accomplishment and identity formation. Although much is taken away, much of value is added to round out the picture of human growth and to 'depathologize' character (cf. Totton 1998: 194–6). But Erikson (1980: 21) also assumes that healthy development equals adaptation to society as it is constituted: 'The growing child must derive a vitalizing sense of reality from the awareness that his individual way of mastering experience . . . is a successful variant of a group identity'.

That 'must' is meant both descriptively and prescriptively. But what happens if group identity and individual needs conflict? As Poster (1978: 70) puts it, Erikson 'simply assumes that the patterns the adults use in raising children have a built-in social wisdom', and then seeks to give advice on how to optimize these patterns.

Conclusion

> It is apparent as I conclude my summary of close on a century of analytic thought about character that there is not an agreed upon definition, not even an agreement about the locus of description.
>
> (Liebert 1989: 58)

As this chapter has shown, Liebert's summary is accurate and reflects, perhaps, the odd overall situation that, although most analysts believe they are all engaged in essentially the same activity, there are almost no specific elements of theory or practice upon which every analyst agrees. Character, then, is just another victim of this unacknowledged general Babel: like the Anglican Church, psychoanalysis is capable of containing an extraordinary range of views and beliefs. However, one of the major analytic theoreticians of character is also one of the few people ever to be actually expelled from the analytic fold, and in the next chapter it is essential therefore to examine the ideas of Wilhelm Reich and his followers.

Reich and his heirs

Character and relationship

Wilhelm Reich's expulsion from psychoanalysis meant that his character theory was developed as part of the body psychotherapy tradition, and often within a humanistic context. His ideas, however, have a firm foundation in psychoanalysis and cannot fully be understood outside it (Totton 1998). Thrashed out in numerous supervision seminars during the 1920s and 1930s, character analysis expanded the original insight of Freud and Abraham into a rigorous and systematic approach to therapy, combined with a general description of human psychic structure, which aspired to connect the personal, familial and social levels.

In a nutshell, Reich believed that character *'serves to maintain the relationship to the outside world and to preserve the psychic equilibrium'* (Reich 1972: 296n, original emphasis). This is a profound formulation, anticipating the more recent emphasis on creative and protective aspects of character structure. Character is above all 'a means of survival': it constitutes 'resistance' not only in the sense of avoidance, but also in its military-political usage, as an organized covert system that eludes and sabotages oppressive forces. Dismantling resistance forces when the liberation struggle ends can be a problem; similarly, a survivor of oppressive early life conditions may find it hard to modify their defensive character structure when it is no longer needed. Beyond its defensive function, a character structure is also a mode of *expression*, a style in which we connect with the world and other people.

Reich (1972: 271) argued that for everyone 'the *first* impulse . . . must be the desire to establish contact with the outer world' (original emphasis). Frustration of this impulse, through prohibition, coldness, avoidance or hostility in those adults with whom there should be a close relationship, produces a structure which, like a symptom, both conceals and presents, expresses and protects our desire. 'A person's character conserves and at the same time wards off the function of certain childhood situations' (Reich 1973: 303). Its specific form will correspond to the libidinal phase at which traumatic frustration is experienced (Reich 1972: 175); for example, oral frustration – deprivation of nurturing and support during the oral 'window' in early childhood – will give rise to a character which in one way or another both *expresses* the need for nurturing and *defends against* it.

In the therapeutic relationship, with its inherent regressive pull, childhood issues are intensely reactivated. The traits that a person uses in life to defend against damage and disappointment are used in therapy to defend against becoming conscious of these buried issues. '*The most important and most conspicuous character trait becomes, in analysis, the most crucial resistance for the purpose of defense*' (Reich 1972: 296n, original emphasis). This is the basis for Reich's major technical innovation: he argued that character issues left unanalysed will sabotage the work – but equally, a deliberate focus on characterological issues will become the fruitful core of therapy.

Bodily aspects of character

> The entire world of past experience was *embodied* in the present in the form of character attitudes. A person's character is the functional sum total of all past experiences.
>
> (Reich 1973: 145, emphasis added)

A theory of character which interprets it as a response to the impact of trauma on the erogenous zones is a *body-centred* theory. The Reichian and post-Reichian concept of character anchors each particular structure in the relational events of developmental life. As we have seen, Reich (1972) argued that libido theory itself, and the erogenous zones in particular, demand that we seek out relationships with others. But our experiences of rejection or aggression are addressed initially to a specific erogenous zone; and to have a structural effect, they must occur while the zone is at the centre of our developmental agenda – during its activation phase, so to speak. Traumas that occur at other periods will colour our character style, but not define its core elements.

There is considerable evidence from neuroscience to support this view.

> A very narrow window – a critical period – exists during which specific sensory experience was required for optimal organization . . . Abnormal micro-environmental cues and atypical patterns of neural activity during critical and sensitive periods, then, can result in malorganization and compromised function in brain mediated functions such as humor, empathy, attachment and affect regulation.
>
> Some of the most powerful clinical examples of this phenomenon are related to lack of attachment experiences early in life.
>
> (Perry *et al.* 1995: 276; cf. Levine 1997;
> Van der Kolk *et al.* 1996)

This picture suggests a potential unification of attachment theory and post-Reichian character theory. As the passage points out, the brain is *mediator* rather than originator of the kinds of changes we are considering (cf. Damasio 1996, 2000): character (or traumatic adaptation) takes place in the bodymind as a whole.

Here we are concerned with what we may call 'non-catastrophic trauma' – relatively tolerable experiences, often interactions with carers, which nonetheless create a style of reaction that limits our freedom. Generally, these are ongoing patterns rather than single events. We might derive character from what Winnicott (1949) calls 'impingements': imperfect elements of caring that demand from the infant or child an effort of adaptation. Winnicott makes it very clear that this is a normal aspect of human development, but at the same time, each demand for such effort reduces the personality's range and flexibility. As John Conger (1994: 95–6) put it:

> Character represents a practice of self-cure, an ongoing, hasty, rigid solution imposed over our instability to maintain an intact sense of self . . . Character is the shell that energy leaves behind, and as such it provides a house; but the shell, as we grow, becomes too small.

As libidinal charge traverses the body in the early years of life, then, it is channelled through a series of more or less successful encounters with the outside world, in the shape of our primary carers. These encounters not only shape our psychic structure; for

Reich and his followers, they also shape our *physical* structure (Lowen 1958). Character can be recognized in the body, before the analysand even speaks. Overall body shape, distribution of muscle and fat, breathing, skin colour and texture, posture, movement style, even metabolic pattern – character is literally *embodied* in all these ways.

Reich's case histories are remarkable for their vivid sense of his analysands' embodiment; he uses these precise descriptions of individuality as a foundation from which to correlate general bodily traits with character structure. Always he moves between the quality of *embodiment* and the quality of psychic presence – Daniel Stern's (1985) 'vitality affects'. Eventually, Reich becomes confident enough systematically to sketch out the bodily features of particular character structures. For example:

> The facial expression and the gait of the hysterical character are never severe and heavy, as they are in the compulsive character; never arrogant and self-confident, as they are in the phallic-narcissistic character. The movements of the archetype have a kind of lilting quality (not to be confused with elastic), are supple and sexually provocative.
>
> (Reich 1972: 205)

This sort of analysis was developed by later Reichians and post-Reichians, and carried well beyond the descriptive level (see in particular Lowen 1958; Kurtz 1990).

Several narratives can be constructed around character as embodiment. We may consider the very specific effects of trauma on the quality of muscle control. For example, the anal sphincter is not under voluntary control in a human infant until the age of several months; emotional pressure from carers to be 'clean' before that age can only be met by tensing the whole gross musculature of the pelvic floor, buttocks, thighs, and so on, with probable long-term damaging effects on the development of fine, precise voluntary use. The overall habitual use of pelvic and associated musculature can be expected to alter the general state of the body, through its indirect effect on functions like blood flow, oxygenation of tissue, elimination of toxins via the lymph system, and so on. The same sort of pattern can occur in any of the body areas identified by Reich (1973) as 'segments' of 'character armour': the head and eyes, mouth and jaw, neck, the chest, the diaphragm, the belly and the pelvis.

Since we spend several years achieving control of our movements, and gross and fine motor control in each muscle group also occurs differentially (Rothwell 1994), voluntary muscle control could be mapped onto a developmental sequence, so that traumatic interaction will appear as a disturbance in specific body areas and affect the final shape and movement and postural style of the adult body. A good deal of work along these lines has already been done, particularly by the Danish 'Bodynamics' group founded by Lisbeth Marcher (Bentzen *et al.* 1996–97; Bernhardt and Isaacs 1997). Several authors have also emphasized the importance of connective tissue, with its plasmatic nature and capacity to shift between rigid and fluid states; the 'schizoid' character structure in particular has been linked to connective tissue disturbances (Davis 1997).

This narrative is not the only one, and perhaps it fails fully to account for the expressive quality of embodied character – how the body *performs* characterological themes, so that, for example, a spindly 'oral' body may powerfully convey lack of support, or a stocky 'anal' body may appear literally 'squashed'. Such perceptions tug us in several different explanatory directions (Totton 1998), each useful in different contexts. The key point is that character is specifically a *quality of embodiment*, an expression of the individual's experience of bodily impulse and its satisfaction or denial.

It is striking that the developmental journey identified by Freud

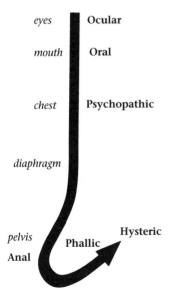

Figure 3.1

and developed by Reich and the post-Reichians is also a journey *through the body*, starting at the head and working downwards to the pelvis. In fact, it follows (Figure 3.1) a specific, curving trajectory down the front of the body, through the diaphragm to the sacrum, and up through the pelvis to the genitals (Totton and Edmondson 1988: 60).

Social aspects of character

Reich's character theory places equal emphasis on the biologically based drives and on object relations in their social context. Character results not from internal conflict, but from external, socially driven frustration of desire:

> The question of why society demands the suppression and repression of drives can no longer be answered psychologically. There are social, more correctly, economic interests that cause such suppressions and repressions in certain eras.
>
> (Reich 1972: 287)

Reich (1972: xxvi) concludes that '*the character structure is the congealed sociological process of a given epoch*' (original emphasis), and that 'every social organisation produces those character structures which it needs to exist' (p. xxii). Social organizations based on authority and exploitation require character structures that can tolerate the pressures this creates. In *The Mass Psychology of Fascism* (Reich 1975), he tried to show how the family mediates the needs of the dominant class to create a pliable and obedient individual character – through sexual inhibition and, more generally, through the inhibition of all forms of pleasure, empowerment and self-expression.

Reich argues that while authoritarian culture depends upon the family instilling a rigid, inhibited and repressed character structure (the 'anal' character being the model), fascism itself appeals to impulses held *below* that tight armour of musculature and character attitudes, which curdle into hate and destruction. The polite, well-behaved surface is separated from 'the deep biological core' by a vicious and violent 'intermediate character layer'.

> In this core, under favourable conditions, man is an essentially honest, industrious, cooperative, loving, and, if motivated, rationally hating animal . . . [But] drop the mask of cultivation,

and it is not natural sociality that prevails at first, but only the perverse, sadistic character layer.

(Reich 1975: 13–14)

Reich insists that 'naturally', 'essentially', human beings are loving, cooperative and rational. Both politically and therapeutically he is an optimist, believing in the realistic possibility of individual happiness, and of social arrangements which are not fundamentally oppressive. But Reich (1972) bases this position on his goal of dissolving neurotic character structure and attaining what he terms 'genitality' and free sexual expression. It is also possible to revalue character more positively and aim for its integration rather than dissolution.

Character as creative

For most contemporary post-Reichians, character is not ultimately about pathology, but about existence as a human being. Each character position defines a *theme*, so to speak. That theme may be existence, nurturing, validation, self-regulation, achievement or meta-communication (each of which corresponds to one of the six basic character types we describe at the end of this chapter). There is nothing pathological about these themes; they will all play themselves out in every life. What determines how harmoniously and creatively they perform is the degree, type and timing of any trauma we encounter in our initial attempts to *express* each theme, and the strategies we therefore adopt to *protect* each theme, even at the cost of disguising or concealing it; together, of course, with whatever work of self-understanding and self-acceptance we may later undertake.

The fundamental quality of each 'character position' (Southgate 1980) can express itself either usefully or damagingly. Each position reflects a developmental stage that we all go through – and all need to go through to attain adult competence and creativity. We all need to be able to 'deal with concrete objects of the material world', as Ernest Jones ([1918] 1977: 437) positively frames the lessons of the anal stage. We all need also to think and imagine ('ocular' stage), to take in nourishment and stand on our own feet ('oral' stage), to use play and fantasy to manage our internal and external objects ('narcissistic' stage), to push ourselves forward and conquer reality ('phallic' stage), and to play, flirt and meta-communicate ('hysteric' stage).

Later developments of Reichian character theory

Through the contributions of many authors, the subject of character has subsequently been deeply explored: its origins and functions, its clinical role, how to recognize it, its expression in body types, and its corresponding metabolic, perceptual, cognitive and neurological types. It has been considered from the point of view of British object relations (e.g. Southgate 1980; Boadella and Smith 1986), ego psychology (e.g. Johnson 1985), classical analysis (e.g. Lowen 1958; Baker 1980), humanistic psychotherapy (e.g. Kelley 1979; Totton and Edmondson 1988; Kurtz 1990), orgonomy (e.g. Baker 1980; Boadella 1987), subtle energetics (e.g. Pierrakos 1987) and therapeutic body-work (e.g. Boyesen 1980; Keleman 1985; Painter 1986).

It is now widely agreed that there are six basic character positions, although various authors name them differently. In addition to the familiar oral, anal and phallic characters of classical psychoanalytic theory, there are the hysteric, the ocular (or schizoid) and the psychopathic. All are seen as normal developmental stages rather than (as the names might seem to imply) pathological structures. Because of this implication, many authors in fact attempt to replace the traditional, pathologizing terms with more neutral or kindly ones: 'ocular' rather than 'schizoid' (Baker 1980), 'tough/generous' rather than 'psychopathic' (Kurtz 1990), 'crisis' rather than 'hysteric' (Totton and Edmondson 1988). The aetiological relationship between character and pathology, although still recognized, is no longer seen as central.

The character types as seen in different schools

Table 3.1 summarizes several post-Reichian character systems, as described by their originators. It follows the 'top to bottom' bodily and developmental sequence that emerges from Reich's work, and tries to give some sense of the relative 'size' and 'position' along this sequence of each character description included: for example, the 'psychopath' position in Bioenergetics includes some of what Reich and Baker described as 'oral' and 'anal'; but some of Reich's 'anal' character, together with some of his 'compulsive' category, is described in Bioenergetics as 'masochistic'.

Table 3.1

Reich (1972) Baker (1980)	Bioenergetics	Hakomi (Kurtz 1990)		Keleman (1985)	Embodied-Relational (Totton and Edmondson 1988)	Related terminology
Ocular *Voyeurist* *Confused*	Ocular	Sensitive/Analytic (containing)			Boundary	*Schizoid* *Borderline*
Oral *Over-indulgent* *Depressive*	Oral	Dependent/Endearing (conserving)	Self-Reliant	Collapsed	Oral	*Dependent* *Addictive* *Depressive*
Anal *Passive-Feminine* *Masochist*	Psychopath *Over-powering* *Seductive*	Tough/Generous (expanding)	Charming/Seductive	Swollen	Control	*Narcissistic* *Charismatic*
Compulsive	Masochistic	Burdened/Enduring		Dense	Holding	*Obsessive*
Phallic-Narcissistic	Rigid	Industrious/Overfocused (producing)			Thrusting	*Type A personality* *Workaholic*
Hysteric *Frantic* *Frozen*	Rigid	Expressive/Clinging (attracting)		Rigid	Crisis	*Histrionic* *Conversion neurosis* *Anxiety*

Working with character

To conclude this chapter, we outline the six basic character positions agreed upon by most modern post-Reichian therapists. Most people are a unique blend of two or more of these character positions. They are identified here by the terminology used in Embodied-Relational Therapy, with some alternative terms added in brackets. The principal body areas are identified (for chakras, see Chapter 6), as well as the principal theme for each position. Three versions of each character position are distinguished:

- the *yearning*, which seeks libidinal satisfaction – corresponding to Fenichel's 'sublimation type';
- the *denying*, which denies the need for satisfaction – corresponding to Fenichel's 'reactive type';
- the *creative*, a successful integration of the character themes into productive life.

The notes also briefly describe the basic therapeutic issues that arise for each character position, including what the person in each position most needs from the therapist, as well as the classic therapeutic 'mistakes' with each position. These 'mistakes', one finds, tend to be irresistibly drawn out of the therapist by particular characters, as part of their need to bring the original trauma to life by reproducing it in therapy. The ways in which each character type may come to grief psychologically are suggested. To flesh out the descriptions, there are lists of typical occupations (though naturally there will be many individual exceptions) and of well-known figures, actual and imaginary, who can be seen as demonstrating each type. In the case of real individuals, the reference is of course to their public role and representation rather than to their private selves.

BOUNDARY POSITION ('schizoid', 'ocular', 'sensitive/analytic')

Womb, birth, bonding. Eye segment block.
Issue: of existence – the right to be.

Yearning version: I need contact, and fear it will destroy/invade/annihilate me. I am less or differently real than other people: I need them to make me real, and fear they will damage my reality still further. I need to understand, to make sense, in order to survive. I need to be born.

Denying version: Only I am real; no-one else truly exists. They are all robots, aliens, fantasies. I have infinite resources in my own mind and imagination; I can complete myself alone. I choose to stay outside the world.

Creative version: I am in touch with the infinite web of realities, with information flow at every level. I can use logic and/or inspiration to connect, to reveal and create pattern, to make sense of the whole. I can stand back without standing outside.

Body

Key areas: eyes and skin. Crown and brow chakras.

Key theme: incompleteness. The body can seem not fully incarnate: unintegrated, immature. Types include the 'professor', awkward, large-headed, dreamy-eyed, stiff-limbed; the pudgy baby; the ethereal elf. Muscles are generally very tense.

Therapy

Contact is experienced as invasive and life-threatening. Therapists must seek to contain the client, as they might hold an eggshell: firmly but very gently, at their boundary but not pressing in against it. The message they need to hear is 'You're welcome here; you can be understood without being invaded; it's safe to meet me, and you can do so on your own terms'.

Classic mistake is to abuse them through mistaking passivity for consent and ignoring the underlying terror. Boundary characters may let therapists do all sorts of things *to* them, while their real self floats away. Most people show boundary characteristics at the beginning of therapy, as they do in many new life situations.

Extreme states

Schizophrenia; autistic spectrum; some forms of dissociation and borderline states.

Typical occupations

Artist; scientist; philosopher; clairvoyant; visionary.

Examples

Spock (Star Trek); Stan Laurel; Sinead O'Connor; Fred Astaire; Joan of Arc; Woody Allen; James Dean; Stephen Hawking.

ORAL POSITION ('dependent/endearing', 'self-reliant')

Feeding, weaning, siblings. Jaw segment block.
Issue: of need – the right to be fed and supported.

Yearning version: I am empty inside, too weak to look after myself. Sometimes I feel I can't go on – the world is bleak and dark. I am never given quite what I want or need. I resent other people's lack of understanding; I know I could be better than all of them given a fair chance.
Denying version: I am strong because I need no-one and nothing. I go through this bleak world alone; like a desert plant, I have formed a tough skin and learned to wait. I will stand up for justice and sometimes may look after others, but inside I despise their weakness – if I could do it on my own, why can't they?
Creative version: I have a robust appetite for life and enjoy taking nourishment in all its forms. I use my eloquence and persuasiveness to get my needs met and also for pure pleasure – and to strive for justice and equality in the world.

Body
Key areas: mouth, throat, wrists and ankles. Throat chakra.
Key theme: lack of support. The body is often undergrounded, with stiff, weak legs and feet; often lanky and ropy – a plant deprived of light – but can be strong and wiry too. Occasionally fat and hungry.

Therapy
For oral characters, therapy, like everything else, is about nourishment and support: they want it, but can't let it happen. Therapists seek to help them admit their need without being thrown into despair, and to tolerate the fact that they will often have to meet their own needs, to self-parent. The message for denying oral characters is 'It's okay to depend on other people sometimes. Your strength is admirable, but we all need help and love'. For yearning orals and deniers who come to admit their need: 'It's true you were unfairly deprived, and nothing can make that up to you; but life is still bearable, sometimes others will support you and sometimes you can support yourself. It's possible to get by'.
Mistakes: to try to feed them, then get angry or depressed when it isn't enough. To resent the denying oral's arrogance.

Extreme states
Depression; bipolar disorder.

Typical occupations
Nurse; cook; orator; beggar.

Examples
Clint Eastwood; Twiggy; Marlene Dietrich; Tony Blair; Judy Garland;
Peter Ustinov; Snow White.

**CONTROL POSITION ('psychopathic', 'tough/generous', 'charming/
seductive', 'swollen', 'charismatic')**

Beginning independence; using adults as play objects. Chest segment
block.
Issue: of validation – the right to be recognized.

Yearning version: I need to be noticed, to have my failures and my
triumphs seen and responded to. I need to be able to get people to
do what I want them to do. I know that I am real, but other people
don't seem to see me – this must be because they aren't real themselves. How can I find someone real who will see me for who I am?
Denying version: I don't need anyone else – trying to relate to
others is weak and stupid. Ultimately there is only myself and what
I want; I have a right to everything if I am strong enough to get it.
Other people are unreal fools, and I enjoy deceiving and manipulat-
ing them.
Creative version: I am a big, powerful person, who needs to relate
actively with others, to make my mark by being useful in the world. I
can afford to give a lot, and get a lot back in approval and recognition.

Body
Key areas: chest and shoulders, arms. Heart chakra.
Key theme: inflation. Chest tends to be puffed up, over-full – but can
be powerful and expansive. Chin tends to be raised, neck stiff, in an
attempt to overawe. There can be a seductive tone.

Therapy
The control character finds it very hard to believe in anyone else's
full reality – still more, to experience trust. The therapist's first task

is to be there, to be real, and to not be manipulated or dominated. If the therapist can keep this up, eventually relationship will be possible. The message for control position characters is: 'You won't dominate or seduce me, but I'm still here for you. I respect your reality and stand up for mine too. You can meet others as equals'.
Mistakes: It's crucial not to lie, whatever the motives. If therapists deny this character's reality, even in positive ways ('things aren't so bad'), it just confirms their expectation. The other major error is to get drawn into dominance games, which are often very subtle.

Extreme states
Sociopathy; some borderline states.

Typical occupations
Gangster; politician; con artist; hostess.

Examples
Bill Clinton; Mae West; Margaret Thatcher; Orson Welles; Mussolini; Wilhelm Reich

---

HOLDING POSITION ('anal', 'masochistic', 'burdened-enduring')

Toilet training, timetabling, pressure to 'behave'. Anal block.
Issue: of regulation – the right to do it my way, in my own time.

Yearning version: I need to let go and push – to splurge, make a mess, spread myself all over things. I want to knead and shape and play with physical matter, to bring my insides outside and admire them. And I'll spoil and crush whatever gets in my way; or sabotage structures with 'mistakes'.
Denying version: I won't – can't – mustn't – let go. I must stick to the rules at all costs, or I'll mess up and be shamed, expose my insides to ridicule; others will be disgusted and reject me. I can only express my anger by forcing others to follow the rules, and by boring and frustrating them.
Creative version: I have the strength to stand for myself, as a natural being in the natural world; the patience to attend to detail, do things the right way, follow through. I am not afraid to be simple, to serve, to get my hands dirty. I follow my own rhythm, and honour the rhythm of all beings.

Body
Key areas: anus, buttocks, thighs, shoulders. Root chakra.
Key theme: containment. The holding body is structured to contain its own energies, to absorb incoming energy and bind it into defensive armouring. Holding characters tend to be stocky, blocky, slab-muscled and well grounded (often good dancers, though not performers). Heads are pulled into the body, eyes sunk into the head.

Therapy
Holding characters are afraid that if they show themselves or act spontaneously, they will be rejected. They demand and resent pressure to perform. (Often they literally ask for physical pressure.) Failure can become a secret revenge – messing up arrangements, forgetting money, not 'getting better'. Holding characters need lots of space, even if they hate it – lots of time, lots of acceptance, to recover their own rhythms, lots of validation at every genuine opportunity. The message to be conveyed to them is: 'I accept you as you are; I want to help you accept yourself, do it for yourself'.
Mistakes: Any sort of pressure from the therapist, whether physical or emotional, is absorbed into and strengthens the armouring. The therapist can easily become the interfering parent, who demands and forbids them to show their insides, who pushes them 'for their own good'.

Extreme states
Masochism; depression; obsessive-compulsive disorder.

Typical occupations
Caretaker; gardener; nurse; bureaucrat.

Examples
Queen Elizabeth II; Spencer Tracey; John Prescott; Marlon Brando; Tina Turner.

THRUSTING POSITION ('phallic', 'industrious-overfocused')

Rebellion, independence, punishment. Pelvic block against softness.
Issue: of assertion – the right to be recognized, to make one's own way.

Yearning version: To feel successful and proud, I will take any risks and defeat any opponent. Life is about working and fighting, excitement and challenge. There will always be another mountain to climb; it's never time to relax and let go, always time to try a little bit harder.

Denying version: Life is dog eat dog – I look out for number one. Feelings are weakening, and I have none. Other people are to be despised and humiliated, especially the opposite sex. I won't enjoy myself and nor will you; if I catch you doing so, I'll smash you.

Creative version: I seek to stretch my abilities, to aspire, do the impossible, test myself against the world. Nothing feels so good as trying my hardest, especially for a worthwhile cause – then basking in my achievement. Life is to be lived and I seek out chances to do so.

Body

Key areas: pelvis, lower back, thighs, shoulders. Sex and solar plexus chakras.

Key theme: uprightness. The thrusting body seeks the vertical at all costs, since anything else threatens collapse. Muscles are rigid and tight with the effort not to fall – resisting any sort of relaxation. There is often an 'inverted triangle' effect – wide shoulders, narrow hips. Athletic, powerful, vulnerable to stress and pain.

Therapy

Surrender, pleasure and closeness are all experienced as humiliating collapse. They mustn't let their guard down. The therapist soon becomes an opponent to be defeated by any means necessary. Instead, therapists can try to model soft strength for them, a tenderness which is not weakness, and help them gradually to enjoy their hidden vulnerability, and to experience fun and enjoyment. The message to be conveyed is: 'Big boys and girls do cry; I respect you for showing your feelings, your softness. Sometimes no-one is on top'.

Mistakes: Rather like control characters, getting drawn into competing – trying to do something clever, to show them who's boss . . . The therapist who wins becomes the therapist who loses. For obvious reasons, few thrusting characters come into therapy – only if they have major psychosomatic symptoms, or if they want to train. The first hurdle to overcome is that they don't have any problems . . .

Extreme states
Sadism; paranoia.

Typical occupations
Athlete; stockbroker; soldier; gambler.

Examples
Arnold Schwarzenegger; Grace Jones; Madonna; Captain Kirk (Star Trek); Tom Cruise.

CRISIS POSITION ('hysteric', 'histrionic', 'expressive-clinging')

Entering the social world, taking on gender. Pelvic block against surrender.
Issue: of contact – the right to choose, to play, to be ambiguous.

Yearning version: It's all too much! Exciting and terrifying things happen all the time. I need your attention, but can't bear to keep still and be really seen. I have to find out the rules in any situation, by breaking them if possible. Everything is sexual, exciting and dangerous.
Denying version: I feel no excitement of any kind; I am passive, the victim of other people's actions. All the excitement and danger is outside me, in other people or in the surrounding situation. Nothing is sexual (but other people keep trying to have sex with me).
Creative version: I can have fun with the rules, while knowing that it's just a game. I can choose in each moment how close to get, and take responsibility for my choices and their effect on others. I love to play, to pretend, to be wild and exaggerated and exciting. There is a sexual side to everything, but it doesn't have to be acted out.

Body
Key areas: pelvis, thighs, chest, eyes. Sex and heart chakras.
Key theme: attraction. The body attracts attention, either by its frequently ripe and full build, or by its graceful, lithe style of movement, which can be very disturbing to others and sometimes to the self. Or the denying style can be completely frozen, awkward and sexless, yet still somehow drawing sexual attention.

Therapy
As with boundary characters, the issue here is mingled desire and anxiety around contact; but the desire is much more charged (sexual) and often active. The crisis character generally keeps approaching,

but at the crunch will do anything rather than simply be present with the therapist. So the strategy is to stay clear of all the fascinating and entertaining material on offer, and to remain in a state of non-judgmental witnessing, to keep pointing out what's going on and bringing them back to face the panic – while still offering a warm and solid human response. The message that needs to be conveyed is: 'I'm not here to meet your needs, and you're not here to meet mine. You can have my attention without performing for it. In this space, you can play without being abused'.

Mistake: Getting sexually involved! More generally, taking it all personally. Their strong feelings about the therapist are mainly a way of avoiding real contact, and lay them and the therapist open to abuse if misunderstood. Crisis material will appear in most people before the end of therapy, although sometimes in very muffled ways. This can be seen as the final stage of the work. Often some apparently urgent reason to leave prematurely will appear – up to and including major illness.

Extreme states
Hysteria; pseudo-schizophrenia; multiple personality; phobia; hypochondria.

Typical occupations
Actor; sex worker; party organizer; pop star.

Examples
Marilyn Monroe; James Dean; Sleeping Beauty; Mick Jagger; David Bowie; Sly Stallone; Bette Davis; Boy George.

Conclusion

Reich is clearly a bridge between psychoanalysis (in its various expressions) and a number of humanistic therapies, some of which would be unlikely allies of classical psychoanalysis. Yet, as we have indicated, to fully appreciate Reich's development of character, it is important to understand its roots in the bodymind developmental sequence which Freud (1905) puts forward as early as *Three Essays on Sexuality*. We have also noted that, in his attempts to develop his own ideas, Reich suffered from that worst characteristic of much of the psychoanalytic movement of the time, its intolerance of apparent deviation from the word of the master.

Although historically Jung precedes Reich, in terms of ideas he represents a greater step away from classical psychoanalytic ideas. Jung, like Reich, was both attracted to Freud's work and at the same time felt the need to develop it in particular directions. Perhaps his development of a typology was a greater break from Freud than Reich's, initiating a different method of classifying character. As in Reich's case, Jung's wish to pursue a particular path led to intense criticism, although perhaps Jung contributed as much to his break with the international psychoanalytic movement as Freud and his immediate circle. Again, like Reich, Jung's development of character and typology acts as a link to other therapeutic approaches, in this case particularly transpersonal psychologies, although transpersonal and Eastern psychologies (as indicated by our reference to chakras in the scheme above) demonstrate interesting links to the bodymind emphasis in Reich. Thus this chapter leads developmentally into Chapters 5 and 6, and Jung's typology similarly links to Chapter 6. It is therefore to Jung's contribution that we now turn.

CHAPTER 4

Jungian typology

A useful tool

In creating his theory of personality types, Jung uses very different
models from the Freudians and Reichians. Characteristically, he aligns
himself with the wisdom traditions of his culture – in this case, the
theory of the four elements, and the corresponding four humours,
which dominated both alchemy and medicine in Europe until the
modern period (see Chapter 6). Jung takes this approach because, in
line with his theory of the collective unconscious (Jung [1959] 1961),
he believes that traditional ways of categorizing the world tend
accurately to reflect our *psychological* structure.

Jung is ambivalent as to how he frames his own typology: Is it
a heuristic device, an objective 'out there' reality, or something
in between? And – a related question – is it a purely psychological
system, or one founded in biochemistry or neurology? On the one
hand, he insists that it is 'not a physiognomy and not an anthro-
pological system, but a critical psychology dealing with the organisation and delimitation of psychic processes that can be shown to
be typical' (Jung [1921] 1971: xv). However, he argues elsewhere:

> The 'humours' of present-day medicine are no longer the old
> body-secretions, but the more subtle hormones . . . The whole
> make-up of the body, its constitution in the broadest sense,
> has in fact a very great deal to do with the psychological
> temperament . . . Somewhere the psyche is living body, and
> the living body is animated matter; somehow and somewhere
> there is an undiscoverable unity of psyche and body.
>
> (Jung [1921] 1971: 542–3)

He goes on in the same work to suggest that personality typology is

> [f]irst and foremost . . . a critical tool for the research worker, who needs definite points of view and guidelines if he is to reduce the chaotic profusion of individual experiences to any kind of order. In this respect we could compare typology to a trigonometric net, or, better still, to a crystallographic axial system.
> (Jung [1921] 1971: 555)

Jung is suggesting that his system is a sort of grid, a set of directions (like North, South, left, right, up, down) superimposed on experience to make it analysable. The question of whether a different grid might be equally effective, or 'true', is not directly answered, although elsewhere he says that his four functions are 'just four viewpoints among many others . . . There is nothing dogmatic about them' (Jung 1978: 49). According to Jung's disciple von Franz, however:

> The question has often been raised: why on earth should there be four functions? why not three? or five? That cannot be answered theoretically, it is simply a question of checking facts and seeing whether one can find more or fewer functions and another typology.
> (von Franz and Hillman 1971: 2)

'Facts', she strongly implies, will support Jung's system: its four-fold nature, and the way in which this corresponds with patterns which appear as 'natural' and meaningful in many cultures, is a function of fundamental psychic structure (Jacobi 1968: 136 ff).

Despite his creation of a character typology, Jung is fairly consistently unenthusiastic about categorizing people: 'Do not think I am putting people into this box or that and saying "He is an intuitive", or "he is a thinking type"' (Jung [1935] 1986: 19). He claims that he used categorization only for practical or persuasive purposes, when he felt the need to explain one person to another to bring them closer together. Attempting to explain what sort of value he sees (and what sort he does not see) in typology, Jung argues that:

> [o]ne can never give a description of a type, no matter how complete, that would apply to more than one individual . . . Classification does not explain the individual psyche. Nevertheless, an understanding of psychological types opens the way to a better understanding of human psychology in general.
> (Jung [1921] 1971: 516)

Despite this, Jung does often refer to people in terms of 'types', and even says that 'the dominating function gives each individual his [*sic*] particular kind of psychology. For example, when a man uses chiefly his intellect, he will be of an unmistakable type' (Jung [1935] 1986: 16). It seems as though, like many of us, Jung enjoyed informally discussing personality types, but when speaking 'on the record' tried to avoid encouraging oversimplification.

The four types

Jung bases his character system on what he identifies as four basic psychological functions, four modes of relating to the world (sometimes identified as 'cognitive modes', or ways of knowing; Loomis 1991: 37). He organizes these four functions in pairs, on two axes, as in Fig. 4.1.

Jung calls the sensation/intuition pair *perceptual* functions, because he considers them to be two equally 'objective' modes of gathering information about reality – one conscious, the other unconscious. The thinking/feeling pair he calls *judging* functions, because he sees them as two modes of evaluating the objective information we have gathered. (Jung also sometimes arranges the four functions as concentric spheres, with sensation as the outermost and closest to the external world, followed by thinking, then feeling and, finally, intuition as the most internally oriented; see Jung [1935] 1986: 47–9).

To make sense of Jung's system we need to understand the rather unusual way in which he is using some of his terms. While sensation represents, as in common usage, information we gather through our senses, including kinesthetic and proprioceptive awareness of our own body, for Jung ([1935] 1986: 14) intuition is 'perception . . . via

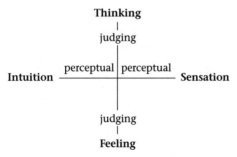

Figure 4.1

the unconscious': an equally objective process to that of sensation. And while thinking means, as we might expect, logical and rational assessment, feeling refers here not to emotion, but to something more like value judgement, aesthetic or moral assessment. For Jung ([1921] 1971: 522; cf. [1935] 1986: 25–7), 'feelings become emotions' only 'when they release physical innervations'.

Jung believes that these four functions usually assert themselves in our personality in combinations, always between *adjacent* functions on the cross or wheel, never between *opposite* ones; that is, never between two judging or two perceptual functions. Thus, for example, thinking can combine with either intuition or sensation, but not with feeling; sensation can combine with thinking or feeling, but not with intuition – the functions are too opposed in nature ever to 'cooperate'. Also, for Jung, each person always has one dominant and well-developed, 'superior' function; while the opposite function to the 'superior' one is always the least-developed, or 'inferior' function (see below). The other two functions, those of the opposite type to the 'superior'/'inferior' pair, become 'auxiliary' functions that may be more or less well-developed; one of these is generally favoured over the other.

> In addition to his [*sic*] main function an individual usually makes use of a second, auxiliary function, which is relatively differentiated and directed. The third function is seldom available to the average man; the fourth, the inferior one, is as a rule entirely beyond the control of his will.
>
> (Jacobi 1968: 13)

Jacobi (1968: 16–17) uses a wheel (Fig. 4.2) to emphasize the intermediate areas *between* functions: 'in actual life the function types almost never appear in pure form, but in a variety of mixed types' (Jacobi 1968: 17).

Perceiving and judging types

Jung's system, therefore, makes a fundamental distinction between two ways of relating to the world: the judging mode and the perceptual mode. He also, rather unfortunately, refers to judging as 'rational' and perceiving as 'irrational' (Jung 1978: 49). The two functions of the perceptual mode, sensation and intuition, do not analyse the external world according to some set of principles, but simply report

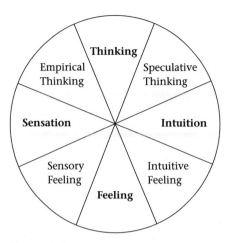

Figure 4.2

on experience. For someone who operates in the perceptual mode, spontaneity and taking life as it comes are predominant qualities; they tend to be open to what *is*, rather than hung up on what *should* be.

Conversely, those in whom the judgement mode of the thinking and feeling functions is dominant tend to prefer structure and organization: they privilege what should be, sometimes over what is. Consistency and predictability are preferred to spontaneity. As we can see, strongly perceptual and strongly judging types often have difficulty understanding and valuing each other's styles; classic examples might be the conflict between hippie and conventional lifestyles, or between Jack Lemmon and Walter Matthau in the movie *The Odd Couple*.

It should also be noted, however, that a 'judging type', for example, will have conscious access only to *one* of the two judging functions: if thinking is superior, feeling will necessarily be inferior and mainly unconscious. At the same time, one of the two perceptual functions, either sensation or intuition, will probably be quite strong and well-developed. Thus most 'judging types' will have a good degree of perception, and most perceptual types a good degree of judgement, even though these are dominated by the superior function.

Extraversion and introversion

As described so far, this system offers eight different basic personality types: superior thinking combined with either sensation or intuition, superior sensation combined with either thinking or feeling, and so on. (The nuances and balances of different functions are, of course, infinitely various, as Jung emphasizes.) However, Jung also distinguishes between two different fundamental orientations or attitudes, which can be expressed through any combination of functions. These he terms *extraversion* and *introversion* (note the 'a' in 'extra' and the 'o' in 'intro'). Jung believes that each human being has an innate, biologically based, preferred orientation, either towards the outer world (extravert) or towards the inner, psychological world (introvert).

Extraverted individuals, then, are oriented towards external reality – sometimes the physical world, sometimes aspects of the human world. They are committed to achievement 'out there', to making a difference through career, through relationships, or through direct labour on the material level. They usually have many friends and connections (often fluid, and easily made and broken), and tend to operate in a group rather than on their own; they are typically active, optimistic and energetic. The weak points of extraversion include a tendency to superficiality and even falseness, which may express itself as an uncritical conventionality.

Introverts, on the other hand, are oriented towards the reality of their own psyche: thoughts, feelings, imagination are what matters to them, and they usually have little concern with how other people value what they produce from within themselves – and little ability to perform according to social expectations, so that their considerable knowledge or abilities are often unknown to those around them. They are not bound by convention and, in fact, tend to react against the general view of things. While extreme extraverts may be in danger of losing their own identity through merging into the collective, extreme introverts run the risk of disconnecting from social and personal bonds altogether, since they tend to dislike large groups and constant interaction. However, these are the extremes, and for most people introvert and extravert elements are combined in their personality in complex ways; however, the extraverted parts of one person will tend to clash with the introverted parts of someone else, and vice versa. [These descriptions are drawn from Fordham (1966) and Loomis (1991).]

According to von Franz, each mode, like the Chinese *yin* and *yang*, unconsciously contains the opposite within itself. Thus for the extravert, 'conscious libido habitually flows towards the object, but there is an unconscious secret counter-attraction back towards the subject'. The introvert, however, 'feels as if an overwhelming object wants constantly to affect him [*sic*], from which he has continually

Table 4.1

Function	Introverted		Extraverted	
	Developed	'Inferior'	Developed	'Inferior'
Sensation	'In touch' with one's body states and rhythms, and with what affects them positively and negatively; stable and consistent perspective	Little sense of one's bodily existence or of what is good or bad for one; hence, stress, illness, eating disorders, etc.	Strong relationship with sensory experience; good perception and memory, intense capacity for enjoyment; grounded and present	Cut off from surroundings and sensory input; pays little attention to appearances; often ignores the obvious
Intuition	Powerfully connected to the unconscious and the world of symbols; capacity for multiple viewpoints and imaginative leaps	Inability to imagine other experiences or points of view	Able to pick up atmospheres and gestalts, to use hunches and to make speculative leaps; attraction to novelty and spontaneity	Difficulty in using imagination to solve problems or envision the future; restricted and negative viewpoint
Thinking	Focus on logical reasoning and problem-solving; concerned to understand and find meaning; focused, self-sufficient and methodical	Inability to think rationally and appropriately; tends towards paranoid constructs and misinterpretations; hard to grasp meaning	Able to think logically and analytically about real-world problems; 'hard-headed', rigorous and efficient	Unable to plan or to see accurate connections between events and phenomena
Feeling	Strong and stable internal value system, unaffected by external pressure; ability to follow one's heart come what may	Undeveloped personal values; difficulty in knowing and expressing what one likes or dislikes; easily swayed	Relationship-centred, sensitive to other people and social situations; empathic, warm, 'people person'	Self-centred, with little empathy or sympathy for others; at the extreme, autistic

to retire; everything is falling upon him, he is constantly over-whelmed by impressions, but he is unaware that he is secretly bor-rowing psychic energy from and lending it to the object through his unconscious extraversion' (von Franz and Hillman 1971: 1).

Table 4.1 shows the various basic combinations of functions and attitudes, and what their implications are for personality style.

The 'inferior function'

A further difficulty of Jung's language arises when we consider the so-called 'superior' and 'inferior' functions. For Jung, it is not so much that the 'superior' function in a particular individual is more valuable, and certainly not that the 'inferior' function is less valu-able. Rather, the superior function is the one *most available for con-scious use*, while the inferior function is least conscious, but by the same token is *most in tune with the unconscious*. In fact, von Franz describes the inferior function as 'the bridge to the unconscious' (von Franz and Hillman 1971: 7), and as 'the door through which all the figures of the unconscious come into consciousness' (p. 54).

Our relation with our inferior function, then, is a difficult one. The inferior function tends to be sensitive and emotionally charged (von Franz and Hillman 1971: 9–11). It does not conform well with the requirements of everyday life, and is 'always associated with an archaic personality in ourselves' (Jung 1935: 21; Quenk 1993). Many people cover up their inferior function with a 'pseudo-adaptation' (von Franz and Hillman 1971: 21; see also below on falsification of type). It can be an Achilles' heel: von Franz says that every German she knew who supported the Nazis in the 1930s was 'caught' by their inferior function (von Franz and Hillman 1971: 66–7). Jung gives the more domestic example of intellectuals who fall foolishly and unsuitably in love (Jung [1935] 1986: 20), an example being the film *The Blue Angel*. Getting in touch with what the inferior func-tion has to offer us is a demanding and risky process, which 'resem-bles an inner breakdown' (von Franz and Hillman 1971: 59). Because it is impossible to 'bring up' the inferior function to the conscious level, we have to let it pull us *down*, via the two intermediate func-tions (von Franz and Hillman 1971: 17).

The inferior function has close connections, therefore, with the Jungian concept of the 'shadow' – the split off and unrecognized side of each person's nature, which, in Jung's view, must be con-sciously integrated as part of the process of growth and individuation.

Similarly, the extravert individual will have an 'introverted shadow' and vice versa (Sharp 1987: 94–100); the inferior function of an extravert will be introverted and vice versa (Sharp 1987: 42–3).

> Encounters with the shadow often coincide with the indi-
> vidual's conscious recognition of the functional and attitudinal
> type to which he belongs. The undifferentiated function and
> under-developed attitude type are our 'dark side', the inborn . . .
> predisposition which we reject for ethical, aesthetic or other
> reasons, and repress because it is in opposition to our con-
> scious principles.
>
> (Jacobi 1968: 110)

Thus Jung dramatically describes the inferior function as 'an open wound, or at least an open door through which anything might enter' (Jung [1935] 1986: 21).

Balancing the functions

Contacting one's inferior function, von Franz suggests, is well worth the trouble, and perhaps a crucial part of the Jungian process of individuation (Jung 1956): it enables us, she says, to overcome 'the tyranny of the dominant function in the ego complex' (von Franz and Hillman 1971: 59), so that we can learn to separate ourselves from all four functions, picking them up and laying them down again like a set of tools, but not identifying with any cognitive mode.

As Jung ([1935] 1986) emphasizes, 'for complete orientation all four functions should contribute equally' (p. 30), although to achieve this perfectly is impossible (p. 109). This is consistent with the central thrust of Jungian thinking, which supports the psychological union of opposites and transcendence of contradictions (Jung 1963). Hence, the creative expression of just one or two functions can never be seen within the Jungian system as a wholly successful adaptation; and the 'inferior function' fills the role within the system of that which trips us up and pushes us into further growth, the inclusion of further functions. 'Everybody thinks his superior function is the top of the world. In that respect we are liable to the most awful blunders . . . no truth can be established without all four functions' (Jung [1935] 1986: 62).

Jacobi describes the sort of crises which result from a one-sided identification with a particular function or attitude:

The neglected functions . . . revolt; they demand their place in the sun, and if all else fails, call attention to themselves by way of a neurosis. For the goal is always psychic totality, the ideal solution in which at least three of the four functions and both reaction types are made as conscious and available as possible.

(Jacobi 1968: 23)

Critiques and developments of Jungian typology

In Anthony Storr's (1973) view, most Jungians, while still using the introversion/extraversion axis, have long abandoned the four functions. Samuels (1985), however, points out that research, both among Jungian analysts and in the literature, does not bear this out. Nevertheless, it would still be fair to say that the theory of psychological types has not played an important part in the development of Jungian psychology, and few major contributions have been made to it since those of Jung himself. This may be at least in part because of a perceived arbitrariness and awkwardness in Jung's system.

In John Heron's (1992) view, for example, although 'the pioneer spirit of holism' in Jung's account of the four functions makes it 'difficult to overestimate its seminal contribution' (p. 192), the theory is 'entirely subverted and distorted by their being defined as species of perceiving and judging' (p. 193). Heron points in particular to the eccentric definitions of feeling and intuition which result from this, and which we have already noted. He observes: 'Of course, people do a lot more with Jung's four functions than his definitions strictly allow. But then they cease to be Jungians and are smuggling in their own more satisfactory phenomenologies' (Heron 1992: 193). Without pretending to be a Jungian, Heron draws on Jung's insights for his own system of four modes, the 'affective', the 'imaginal', the 'conceptual' and the practical', which we look at further in Chapter 6.

A good example of the type of Jungian revisionism to which Heron refers might be the work of Mary Loomis, who 'improves' Jung in ways that deeply change his theory of the four functions.

The oppositional arrangement of the functions as imaged by the cross was a teaching device used by Jung to explain the possible interaction of the functions. Unfortunately, it has contributed to the misunderstanding of Jung's theory . . . The

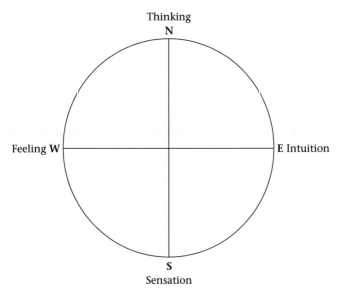

Figure 4.3

oppositional arrangement contradicts Jung's basic premise that the aim of psychological growth is the resolution of contradictions.

(Loomis 1991: 31)

Loomis combines Jung's description with the Native American Medicine Wheel approach (see Chapter 6), which repeatedly uses a cross inscribed within a circle as a fundamental structure for organizing many different sorts of material. To correspond with the qualities of the four directions within the Native American system, the ordering of the four functions has to change, so that Thinking opposes Sensation and Feeling opposes Intuition. Loomis describes how, in this revised wheel of the functions, interaction is possible both between adjacent functions (e.g. sensation and feeling) and between opposite functions (e.g. sensation and thinking). 'Mental faculties need not be limited to an interaction between one perceiving and one judging function, as Jung originally hypothesised' (Loomis 1991: 451; cf. Singer 1995: 345–51).

Metzner (1981) went even further in his revision of Jung's system, denying the superior/inferior/auxiliary pattern altogether, and replacing it with a twelve-fold typology where the four functions can be combined in any order. Like Loomis, he questions the value of the traditional cross-circle arrangement of the functions, and also suggests replacing the terms 'perceiving' and 'judging' with 'experience' and 'judgement of experience'.

Jungian personality inventories

Whatever their role in Jungian analysis, the Jungian personality types have been highly influential in the psychology of personality, in particular Jung's basic distinction between introversion and extraversion (Mattoon 1981: 56–61). The Myers-Briggs personality inventory (MBTI), which measures an individual's use of the Jungian four functions and two modes (Myers 1962), has been an important force in popularizing Jungian typology. It is widely used by psychologists and as the basis for several 'pop' approaches to personality typing. Something like one million people are said to have undergone the MBTI in 1986 alone (Sharp 1987: 93). Many people find the 16 MBTI types highly meaningful to them: there are even clubs and discussion groups for those with the same type!

Loomis suggests, however, that both the MBTI and the Gray-Wheelwrights Jungian Type Survey (Wheelwright *et al.* 1964) are victims of their own assumptions: Jung's hypothesis (that the 'superior' and 'inferior' functions will always be paired opposites on the function wheel, so that, for example, superior thinking necessarily equates with inferior feeling) is built into the way in which the questions are constructed and, therefore, inevitably emerges from the answers (Loomis 1991: 44).

Together with June Singer, Loomis has revised the existing inventories, substituting scaled-response for forced-choice questions, thus allowing a more open pattern to emerge. Loomis and Singer found that 61 per cent of subjects had a different 'superior' function on the revised inventory from that given by the MBTI or Grey-Wheelwright, while 48 per cent no longer had an 'inferior' function opposite their 'superior' one (Loomis 1991: 45–6). They went on to construct a new Jungian inventory, the Singer-Loomis Inventory of Personality (SLIP) (Singer and Loomis 1984), which independently measures each of the eight Jungian types (introverted sensation, extraverted sensation, etc.) through scaled-choice questions and then combines these into an overall picture. Loomis (1991), in parallel with contemporary post Reichians (Chapter 3), emphasizes both the creative aspects of each function type, and the possibility and desirability of exploring one's own less-developed functions.

Falsification of types and the physiology of Jungian typology

Katharine Benziger emphasizes the concept, found in Jung's original work, of the 'falsification of type': for a number of reasons – family or group pressure, for example – individuals can unknowingly mis-represent their own personality type, living in a style which causes them great difficulty and stress. As Jung ([1921] 1971: 425) puts it, 'whenever such falsification of type takes place as a result of external influence, the individual becomes neurotic later, and a cure can successfully be sought only in the development of the attitude which corresponds with the individual's natural way'. Benziger (1995) suggests that a specific syndrome, Prolonged Adaptation Stress Syn-drome (PASS), arises from chronic falsification of type. She has done useful work generally in relating Jung's typology to the findings of modern neuroscience, and identifying the physiological corollaries of the different types (Benziger 1996).

Hillman's radical orthodoxy

The distinguished Jungian analyst James Hillman, whose work on the feeling function we have already considered, has written very critically of the conventional ways in which Jung's personality typing is understood (Hillman 1980). Hillman claims to return to Jung's original intentions, although such claims to restore the original purity of any system are usually to be suspected. However, Hillman makes a good case, pointing out that Jung explicitly denies any intention of typecasting individuals (e.g. Jung [1921] 1971: 554–5). It is, how-ever, equally true that Jung spends quite a lot of time doing exactly what he denies believing in (Jung [1921] 1971: Ch. 10).

Hillman distinguishes strongly between the concept of 'types', which he regards as essentially fluid and mixed, and the more rigid and exclusive concept of 'classes', with which he believes types have become confused. In the terms we used in Chapter 1, he is arguing in other words that Jung's types are properly *fuzzy* categories but have become misunderstood as *tight* ones. In this and other recent works (e.g. Hillman 1996), Hillman is trying to reinstate a very tra-ditional conception of character as the essence of individual unique-ness, and to relate it to concepts like 'fate' and 'purpose'. He argues that therapy would be best advised to abandon questions about child-hood causation in favour of questions about meaning and goal, like 'what does my angel want with me?' (Hillman and Ventura 1992: 70).

Social and political implications

Work on the social implications of Jungian typology has focused mainly on the role of the 'inferior function' as the bearer of unassimilated unconscious material (cf. Quenk 1993) and, in particular, on the significance of the fact, as Jung saw it, that in our culture as a whole it is the *feeling* function that is inferior (von Franz and Hillman 1971: 104). Bratherton (1998: 184) describes this as 'the main wound of modern society', partly because of its differential effects on men and women and the wedge that it helps to drive between them. The inferior feeling function tends to be identified with women, contributing to their positioning as marginal and inferior. As Hillman puts it, 'It is in fact one of the insidious clichés of our time (and one which Jungian psychology has not done enough to dispel) that eros and feeling have an affinity with women' (von Franz and Hillman 1971: 97).

For Robert Johnson (1993: 9), 'men and women suffer quite differently from the wounding of their feeling functions and much of the tension and lack of communication between man and woman springs from this difference'. This difference itself is, of course, a function of differential treatment of the sexes, and Jungians (like many others) are perhaps vulnerable to circular thinking in this area. Feminists have frequently critiqued Jung's view of women (Wehr 1987; Young-Eisendrath and Weidemann 1987), which includes many of his observations on the four functions in relation to gender. An important perception to emerge out of Jungian work in this area, however, is that – no doubt for culturally enforced reasons – men tend to project their own feeling function onto women, and women tend to project their thinking function onto men, in ways which are damaging to both. Young-Eisendrath and Weidemann (1987) base much of their approach to feminist Jungian therapy on the need for women to reclaim their own authority, including their capacity to think, from the social and cultural locations on to which they have projected it.

We have already noted Marie von Franz's view that Germans seduced by Nazism were 'caught' by their inferior function. If accurate, this observation has enormous social implications, and makes the development of the inferior function in everyone a matter of serious urgency. What sort of political practice might follow from this, especially combined with von Franz's other observation that groups tend to 'share out' the functions between them? Perhaps such ideas have influenced the work of Arnold Mindell, originally a Jungian analyst, who teaches and practises World Work, a form of large group interaction with the goal of taking back projections, and celebrating the sharing-out of perceptions and reactions in a process of 'deep democracy' (Mindell 1992).

Conclusion

Jung's typology, like his general analysis of personality structure (see the companion volume in this series by Brinich and Shelley), clearly has a wide popular appeal. The same could be said of his notion of archetypes, which have also been used as a basis for personality typing. Through his work on symbolic aspects of the psyche, Jung concludes that the unconscious contains a relatively small number of 'centres and fields of force' (Jacobi 1968: 42), which express themselves throughout all cultures in characteristic imagery – often personified as human characters, such as the Mother, the Child, the King, and so on. As Jacobi (1968: 47–8) suggests: 'In every single individual psyche they can awaken to new life, exert their magical power, and condense into a kind of "individual mythology"'. As we shall see in Chapter 6, it is possible to develop personality systems based on the role played by different archetypes in different individual psyches, although such systems are vulnerable to the common popular misunderstanding of the archetypes as like a series of Olympian gods and goddesses whose features are mirrored in human beings.

Jung's ideas seem to lend themselves to various forms of popularization, with all its attendant dangers. They seem readily to be pulled into the gravitational field of conventionalized New Age thinking, however rigorous they may be in their pure form, and when employed by Jungian analysts. In the various ways described in this chapter, Jung and his followers clearly make an important contribution to typology. In Chapter 6, we shall also see, in addition to archetypes, how two other features of Jung's work – his attention to spirituality and to Eastern philosophies – have influenced transpersonal typologies.

Humanistic and research-based typologies

Unwilling acquiescence

Humanistic therapy has tended strongly to question the role of personality typing. Carl Rogers, for example, argued consistently against the use of diagnostic categories, on the grounds that if the client 'perceives the locus of judgement and responsibility as clearly resting in the hands of the clinician, he is ... further from therapeutic progress than when he came in' (Rogers 1956: 223). Other Rogerian writers have supported this view, stating that person-centred therapy essentially treats all clients in the same way, and that therefore diagnosis and assessment are meaningless (Shlien 1989), and arguing that the person-centred viewpoint on this should be taken into account by the psycho-practice professions (Boy 1989). For the person-centred therapist, each client is their own unique 'type', using their own 'personal language' as an individually characteristic way of expressing themselves (Mearns and Thorne 1992).

Person-centred therapy, however, also provides examples of a significant trend in humanistic therapy towards acceptance of diagnostic typing – not on theoretical grounds, but essentially because of social and professional pressure to assess and diagnose. For example, Bozarth (1998), while stating categorically that 'psychological assessment as generally conceived is incongruent with the basic assumptions of client-centred theory' (p. 127), goes on to point out that 'tests and assessment are increasingly used for the agency, institution, insurance payment determination, or reasons other than understanding clients', and to argue that 'the person-centred counsellor working in this kind of setting must adjust (even be "empathic") to the system to survive' (p. 128). In the same way, it is not unusual, for example, to find Gestalt therapists using DSM IV categories in constructing a picture of the client, or other forms of typology (see below) that assist the therapist in identifying risks as well as potential areas upon which to focus with the client.

There is a degree of special pleading in the use of the Rogerian term 'empathic' to justify what is arguably a breach of faith in the interests of survival. Similarly, Clarkson uses a perhaps over-subtle logic to support the same sort of acquiescence in a Gestalt context:

> The counsellor using the Gestalt approach will be forever questioning the assumptions underlying the use of diagnostic categories. Equally, he or she will also regularly question the assumptions underlying the rejection of diagnostic categories.
> (Clarkson 1989: 57)

The reality is that both Rogerian and Gestalt therapy were originally flatly opposed to any sort of fixed typological categories, and that both have compromised on the issue basically because of the need to bow to institutional forces.

Gestalt: unfinished business

What is equally true, however, is that Fritz Perls was throughout his life consciously indebted to Reichian conceptions of character, and that he worked his own version of character theory into his new system. (Most post-Reichian therapies are, of course, humanistic in tone, but we have treated them separately since their theoretical ground is very different.) Perls ([1955] 1975: 4) recognizes that 'the formation of character' allows the individual to 'act only with a limited, fixed set of responses', and he classifies types of such limited responses as five different interruptions of the cycle of creativity. However, Perls repeatedly insists that this scheme 'is not a classification of neurotic persons but a method of spelling out the structure of a *single* neurotic behaviour' (Perls *et al.* 1973: 518). In other words, in Perls' view, each person uses all these interruptions at different points in the cycle. Instead of trying to identify and treat 'the "real" underlying character that the therapist guesses at . . . we need only help the patient develop his creative identity by

Table 5.1 (based on Clarkson 1989)

Interruption	Place in creativity cycle	Issues
Desensitization	Sensation	Avoids experiencing self or environment
Deflection	Awareness	Avoids contact
Introjection	Mobilization	Internalized 'should's'
Projection	Action	Disowned qualities are attributed to others
Retroflection	Final contact	Doing to self what one wants to do to others/get from others
Egotism	Satisfaction	Self-observation narcissism
Confluence	Withdrawal	Merges with others

his ordered passage from "character" to "character"' (Perls *et al.* 1973: 508–509).

There is a great temptation, however, to adjust this schema into a character typology; indeed, there is a good deal of logic in doing so, given Perls' acknowledgement that there *are* fixed character structures each with its own stereotyped responses. Clarkson, for example, while explicitly cleaving to Perls' position against typology, links several of the interruptions to standard diagnostic categories – for instance, she compares confluence with borderline personality disorder (Clarkson 1989: 51–7) – and describes them as potentially 'chronically or acutely pathological' (p. 45). She uses Perls' original five interruptions with the addition of the two further phenomena of deflection and desensitization, which are described by some Gestalt therapists (Table 5.1).

It would not, in fact, be hard to assign a diagnostic label to each interruption: 'schizoid' to Desensitization and Deflection, 'oral' to Deflection and Introjection, 'paranoid' to Projection, 'masochistic' to Retroflection, 'narcissistic' to Egotism and 'borderline' to Confluence, perhaps? Such a suggestion represents the sort of integration of ideas from different therapies to which Clarkson herself is strongly committed. We return to the idea of integrating personality typologies in Chapter 7.

Maslow's hierarchy of needs

Although Maslow, one of the founding figures of humanistic psychotherapy, is also hostile to formal diagnostic categories – because they imply that 'the person who comes to the counselor is a sick person . . . seeking a cure' (Maslow 1971: 51) – his concept of the 'hierarchy of needs' can be used as the basis of a personality typology. Like Rogers, Maslow (1968: 33) believes in an innate tendency to growth: 'what a man *can* be, he *must* be'. However, he stresses the word 'can' in this sentence, and points out that a certain orderedness applies here: there are basic needs that must be met before more subtle needs can be either experienced or satisfied. For example, 'in the choice between giving up safety or giving up growth, safety will ordinarily win out' (Maslow 1968: 49).

Maslow's basic hierarchy is shown in Fig. 5.1. Here, each 'lower' need must be met before the next level of need can come into focus. Maslow devotes considerable time to exploring his ruling concept of self-actualization, breaking it down into a number of different 'metaneeds', including beauty, truth, goodness and justice; he also gives examples of a somewhat narrow range of self-actualizing individuals, including Thomas Jefferson, Albert Einstein and Eleanor Roosevelt. For Maslow, the lower the point on the pyramid where someone's needs are frustrated, the more serious the pathology they will display. Focus on different levels of the pyramid of needs will give rise to different personality types.

A great strength of Maslow's approach is that it intrinsically brings in the social and political aspects of reality. On the one hand, social

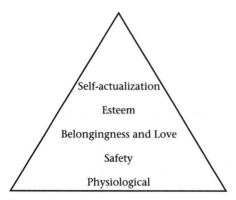

Figure 5.1 (based on Maslow 1968)

conditions will largely determine the extent to which particular needs are satisfied, and hence the balance of personality types within a given society; on the other hand, the theory gives direct support to campaigns for improving social conditions, since only in this way can psychological health be attained. It also implicitly demonstrates the weakness of programmes to make psychotherapy available to disadvantaged groups. It questions whether psychotherapy can be of any use to them until their needs for food, shelter, and so on are met. Counsellors and therapists working in settings offering subsidized therapy often find that there are basic needs problems – such as low income and spiralling debt, housing problems, or training and educational issues – where it is essential for effective therapy that some of these issues are addressed, either by the therapist or by referral to specialist resources.

Transactional Analysis

Originally, Transactional Analysis (TA) was resistant to psychopathology and to characterology in general, along the same lines as other humanistic therapies; however, social and political pressures have led to the adoption of the usual 'DSM' diagnostic categories. Together with this, the general appeal for many TA practitioners of neat and tidy structures, catchy terminology and clear clinical strategies has powered the development of some specifically TA-inflected ideas about personality types.

Although the fundamental TA distinction between the three ego states of Parent, Adult and Child (Berne 1968) could easily be used as the basis of a personality typing along the lines of the 'libidinal types' suggested by Freud (1931), this line of thought has not in practice been developed. One quite simple typology that is used in TA, however, is based on Eric Berne's famous 'OK–Not OK' concept, which gives rise to four positions: 'I'm OK, You're OK' (regarded as healthy), 'I'm OK, You're not OK' (linked to paranoid personality), 'I'm not OK, You're OK' (linked to the depressive personality) and 'I'm not OK, You're not OK' (described as the 'futility position': Stewart and Joines 1987: 119–21). These four positions are linked by Ernst (1973) with four 'operations': in the same order they are 'Get-on-with', 'Get-rid-of', 'Get-away-from' and 'Get-nowhere-with'.

This represents a set of four basic 'life scripts', or fundamental beliefs and styles of conducting oneself. The concept of the life script is a

Table 5.2 (based on Stewart and Joines 1987: 155–8)

Driver	Words	Tone	Gestures	Posture	Expression
Be Perfect	Often uses qualifiers and parentheses	Well-modulated; 'adult sounding'	Counting off points on fingers; stroking chin; steepling fingers	'Adult-looking'; upright	Looking upwards or to side while speaking, as if trying to read off the right answer
Please Others	Often uses 'but' and question structures	High, squeaky, rising at end of sentence	Reaching out, palms up; nodding	Shoulders hunched and forward, leaning forwards	Looking 'up from under'; eyebrows raised; tense smile
Try Hard	Uses words like 'try', 'difficult', 'can't'	Muffled, strangled voice	Hand to eyes/ears, as if straining to see/hear	Hunched, strained forward	Vertical frown above nose; face screwed up
Be Strong	Distancing words like 'one', 'you', 'people'; use of passive constructions	Flat, monotonous, low	Absence of gestures	Closed posture, e.g. folded arms, crossed legs	Expressionless; immobile
Hurry Up	'Hurry', 'quick', 'no time . . .'	Staccato, rushed	Finger and foot tapping; wriggling around	Overall agitated	Frequent rapid shifts of gaze

Table 5.3 (based on Berne 1973: Ch. 5; Kahler 1978: 60–5; Stewart and Joines 1987: 148–62

Process script	Motto	Primary driver
until	'I can't have fun until . . .'	Be Perfect
after	'I'll have to pay for it after . . .'	Please Others
never	'I can never get what I most want'	Be Strong
always	'Why does this always happen to me?'	Try Hard
almost, Type 1	'I almost made it'	Please Others + Try Hard
almost, Type 2	'This is almost good enough'	Please Others + Be Perfect
open-ended	'What now?'	Please Others + Be Perfect

rich source of further forms of personality typing. It is theorized that the variety of life scripts are all generated by different combinations of five basic instructions, or 'drivers': Be Perfect, Be Strong, Try Hard, Please (People) and Hurry Up (see Table 5.2). These reflect a position of 'conditional OKness' (Stewart and Joines 1987: 163): in other words, there is a parental message that 'you are OK if and only if you do this'. Drivers can be recognized not only from the content of a person's material, but from their choice of wording, gestures, expressions, tone of voice etc.

Transactional Analysis further identifies six 'process scripts' – life patterns that people appear to create and perpetuate unconsciously – that relate to the five drivers: 'Whether I am Chinese, African, or American, I will live out my script according to one or more of these six patterns. The same is true whatever my age, sex, education or culture' (Stewart and Joines 1987: 148). These process scripts (one of which has two subforms) are generated from combinations of the drivers, as shown in Table 5.3.

Stewart and Joines (1987: 163–4) emphasize that there is as yet no clear theory of the causality of this system:

Why are there five and only five driver behaviors? Why are they the same for everyone, regardless of culture, age or education? . . . Nobody knows. . . . One of the most challenging tasks of current TA research is to produce a convincing account of the origins of driver behavior.

Table 5.4 (based on Ware 1983)

Adaptation	Characteristics	Description	Drivers	Injunctions
Schizoid	Withdrawn, passive, day-dreaming, avoidant, detached	Shy, over-sensitive, eccentric	Be Strong, Try Hard or Please Others	Don't Make It; Don't Belong; Don't Enjoy; Don't Be Sane; Don't Grow Up; Don't Feel (Love, Sex, Joy); Don't Think
Hysterical	Excitable, unstable, over-reacting, dramatic, attention-getting, seductive	Immature, self-centred, vain, dependent	Please Me, Try Hard or Hurry Up	Don't Grow Up; Don't Be Important; Don't Think
Obsessive-compulsive	Conformist, conscientious	Perfectionist, inhibited, over-conscientious, over-dutiful, tense	Be Strong + Be Perfect	Don't Be a Child; Don't Feel (Joy and Sex); Don't Be Close; Don't Enjoy
Paranoid	Rigid thinking, grandiose, projecting	Hyper-sensitive, suspicious, envious, jealous	Be Strong + Be Perfect	Don't Be a Child; Don't Feel; Don't Be Close; Don't Enjoy
Antisocial	Socially conflictual, intolerant of frustration, needs excitement	Selfish, callous, irresponsible	Be Strong + Please Others	Don't Make It; Don't Be Close; Don't Be a Child; Don't Feel
Passive-aggressive	Aggressive, resentful	Obstructive, stubborn, difficult	Try Hard + Be Strong	Don't Feel, Don't Be Close, Don't Enjoy It; Don't Make It

In the assessment of clients, the drivers and script patterns are combined with a set of twelve (or more) 'injunctions': inhibitions on behaviour that can be expressed in the form of statements beginning 'Don't'. These are: Don't Be, Don't Be You, Don't Be A Child, Don't Grow Up, Don't Make It, Don't (Do Anything), Don't Be Important, Don't Belong, Don't Be Close, Don't Be Well (or Sane), Don't Think and Don't Feel (Goulding and Goulding 1972; Stewart and Joines 1987: Ch. 14).

This chilling list can be dealt with by the individuals who internalize them in several ways. One of these is to 'antidote' an injunction with a driver – for example, Don't Exist with Work Hard, so that the script is 'So long as I work hard, it's OK for me to stay alive' (Stewart and Joines 1987: 142). Although drivers are basically verbal in nature, and can sometimes be 'heard' repeating themselves inside our heads, injunctions are essentially preverbal, and were originally conveyed to us behaviourally by our carers (Stewart and Joines 1987: 133).

Several authors have used these ideas in various ways as building blocks for their own syntheses. Paul Ware (1983) takes six personality types from traditional pathology and assigns to each a set of drivers and a set of injunctions (Table 5.4). To help the therapist approach these six types, Ware assigns to each a 'contact door' – in other words, an initial point of access through an area where that type invests its energy; a 'target door', or new but attainable area of investment; and a 'trap door', an area to be avoided until later in the therapy (see Table 5.5). Ware (1983: 18) claims that 'effective therapists have been following these processes for a long time, at an intuitive or an unconscious level'.

Table 5.5   (based on Ware 1983)

Adaptation	Contact door	Target door	Trap door
Schizoid	Behaviour	Thinking	Feeling
Hysterical	Feeling	Thinking	Behaviour
Obsessive-compulsive	Thinking	Feeling	Behaviour
Paranoid	Thinking	Feeling	Behaviour
Antisocial	Behaviour	Feeling	Thinking
Passive-aggressive	Behaviour	Feeling	Thinking

Joines (1986) enthusiastically takes up Ware's system into his own sub-brand of TA, Redecision Therapy. However, he points out (similarly to several post-Reichians; see Chapter 3) that 'a person can manifest any of these adaptations and be healthy or anywhere on the traditional continuum of psychopathology. Thus, the adaptations imply neither health nor pathology' (Joines 1986: 153). Hence he renames the six types as follows: Creative Daydreamers for schizoids, Brilliant Sceptics for paranoids, Charming Manipulators for antisocials (perhaps not such a value-neutral name?), Playful Critics for passive-aggressives, Responsible Workaholics for obsessive-compulsives, and Enthusiastic Overreactors for hysterics. He also discusses combination types, and brings in the TA ego states in more detail in discussing treatment approaches.

As so often with TA, these approaches to personality typing raise the question: Is this a system, or simply a set of brilliant and plaus-ible epigrams shoehorned into a formal structure? Two things are perhaps lacking from TA's personality typologies. As Stewart and Joines (1987: 163–4) acknowledge, there is no place for causality in the system – it just *is*. The same is true of a number of other typologies, for example Jung's; but TA does not take the alternative path of giving its system a formal patterning that carries its own conviction. Also missing is a sense of deep structure – it is not clear that the TA categories are actually deeper than the information they organize, rather than simply on the same level. The very elaborate-ness and eloquence of the TA approach highlights this absence of explanatory power.

Research-based typologies

We also need to consider in this section some contributions to personality typing that come from psychological or neuro-scientific sources, and which have been taken up by humanistic therapists and counsellors – often not in a particularly precise way, but more as iconic representations of 'the backing of science' for ideas that are not themselves necessarily scientific.

Left brain, right brain

An excellent example of this is the dichotomy between 'left brain types' and 'right brain types' (Ornstein 1977), deriving from the extraordinary effects of surgical operations to cut the corpus callosum in the brains of people suffering from severe epilepsy. This has the effect of cutting communication between the left and right hemispheres of the brain, leading to the unexpected discovery that the two hemispheres are capable of operating 'independently' and even antagonistically – but also, that they operate in significantly different ways (Gazzaniga 1970).

The differences between the modes of operation of the hemispheres have been described in a number of different ways, including (with the left-sided characteristic first in each case) verbal *vs* non-verbal, logical *vs* intuitive, intellectual *vs* aesthetic, linear *vs* holistic and temporal *vs* spatial (Pelletier 1978; Springer and Deutsch 1985). Given that the left hemisphere controls the right side of the body and vice versa, this conforms closely with traditional distinctions between the right and left sides of the body (Bogen 1975). Ornstein (1977) has even equated the left brain with consciousness and the right brain with the unconscious.

Popularizers and visionaries (Ferguson 1973; Buzan 1976; Jaynes 1976) have turned these differences into a set of ideas about 'two different forms of consciousness', and then 'two different kinds of people', each specialized in one of these forms. The term 'dichotomania' has been used to describe this flood of speculation (Springer and Deutsch 1985), which, of course, ignores the fact that, in virtually everyone, the two hemispheres are *not* separated from each other, but are in constant cooperation.

> The brain is adapted to create and maintain human society and culture by two complementary conscious systems. Specialized motives in the two hemispheres generate a dynamic partnership between the intuitive, on the one side, and the analytic or rational, on the other side, in the mind of each person.
>
> (Trevarthen 1987: 746)

It would appear, then, that 'left brain/right brain' is primarily used in therapy and counselling as a contemporary scientific gloss on traditional folk-psychology ideas about two cognitive styles. In rather the same way that Jung describes using his typology as a way of helping people understand and accept each other's differences, 'left brain' and 'right brain' can be used to facilitate relations between individuals with very different preferred styles of thinking and interacting. Things start to get trickier, and hotter, when a 'hemispheric politics' is introduced, with the idea that our society is 'left brain dominant' and that 'left brain' is then aligned with 'rational', 'patriarchal' and 'male'.

Styles of learning

A more complex and subtle approach to cognitive styles is the set of seven types of intelligence offered by Howard Gardner (1983; Armstrong 1987). Gardner suggests that society currently recognizes and values only two or three of the seven kinds of intelligence which he identifies. Linguistic, logical-mathematical and intrapersonal intelligence are celebrated, but far less status attaches to musical, bodily-kinaesthetic, spatial and interpersonal intelligence ('intrapersonal intelligence' refers to what Jung would term an introverted intuitive type). Clearly, some of these talents could be defined in other ways than as 'intelligence'; but this is in fact Gardner's central point – that the word 'intelligence' is given an artificially restricted meaning in line with society's restricted valuation of talents.

Although each of us has all seven forms of intelligence in some proportion, those proportions vary – sometimes to an extreme degree. Such differences characterize not only the areas in which each person is likely to shine, but also the styles in which each person will be most able to *learn*. Thus individuals with intelligence of a socially-central kind are doubly privileged: not only are they praised and valued, but they are also taught in a style which they find easy to assimilate, whereas other young people are not only made to feel less valued in themselves, they are also taught in what amounts to a foreign language. For example, children – and adults – whose intelligence is bodily-kinaesthetic need opportunities to learn by moving and acting things out. Without such opportunities, they are vulnerable to being labelled as 'hyperactive' and possibly given damaging drug treatment.

What are the applications of these ideas to psychotherapy and counselling? Their most obvious value is reparative, in providing a framework for rebuilding the self-esteem of the many people who have been wounded by their experience of education: helping them realize that the failure was not theirs, but that of the school system. They also provide a framework – one of several described in this book – for enabling therapists to adjust their own communicative style to better match that of each of their clients.

Sheldon's somatotypes

A rather different sort of typology is William Sheldon's (1942) system for relating physique and temperament, which has migrated from psychology into widespread use by therapists and counsellors – although, like the hemispheric approach, it appears more as a diffuse background idea than as a precise tool for understanding. Also like the hemispheric approach, Sheldon's system takes up and supports the folk psychology of body types – that fat people tend to be relaxed and sociable, thin people tense and thinking-oriented, and muscular types active and assertive. However, Sheldon's distinction between endomorphs (soft, well-rounded, tending to fat), mesomorphs (muscular, sturdy and tough) and ectomorphs (slender, fragile and flat-chested) is based on research – the analysis in the first instance of four thousand individuals – and is also more subtle than a simple tripartite division. Sheldon uses a 7-point scale for each dimension, so that a 7-1-1 individual will be a 'pure' endomorph, a 5-2-2 individual will have strong endomorphic tendencies, and so on. This yields a total of 343 different body types.

The temperaments which, for Sheldon, correspond with each of his three central physical types are as follows. The endomorphic person is *viscerotonic*: that is, dominated by their guts – in traditional terms, a phlegmatic Earth temperament (for the traditional elemental system, see Chapter 6). The mesomorphic type is *somatotonic*: muscle oriented and in love with action, a choleric Fire temperament. And the ectomorph is *cerebrotonic*: brain-centred, hyperattentive and inhibitory, a melancholic Water temperament. It is interesting to note that there is no type corresponding to the Air element: perhaps the somatotypes are closer to the three-fold Ayurvedic distinction between sattva, rajas and tamas (pp. 93–7).

These three psychophysical types can also be related to the tripartite archaic division of embryonic tissue: the *endoderm* that eventually forms the viscera, the *mesoderm* that will become muscle and bone, and the *ectoderm* that will become brain, nervous tissue and skin (Grossinger 1986). These three layers are also central to David Boadella's post-Reichian characterology and therapy (Boadella 1987). From these basic differentiations, Sheldon weaves a complex and plausible set of mixed-type character portraits. Most people are clearly of mixed types: the endomorphic mesomorph is solid and powerful, the ectomorphic mesomorph wiry and muscular, the ectomorphic endomorph spread out and rounded without being muscular, and so on.

Table 5.6 (based on Sheldon 1942; O'Hanrahan 1999)

	Body system	Keyword	Physique	Temperament	Therapy approach
Endomorph	Digestive system and viscera	Comfort	Large, rounded, soft	'Viscerotonic': tends to friendliness, laziness, peacefulness, dependence, lack of discrimination	Give plenty of time; avoid pressure; encourage autonomy
Mesomorph	Muscles, circulation and skeleton	Action	Large, strong, muscular	'Somatotonic': tends to physical activity, assertiveness, competition, unsubtlety, aggression	Can be confronted forcefully; work in short 'bites'; encourage softness
Ectomorph	Nervous system including brain	Detachment	Thin, wiry, fragile	'Cerebrotonic': tends to intellectuality, tension, withdrawal, fearfulness, quickness	Approach carefully and gently; do not overload; encourage slowing down and body awareness

Sheldon's explanatory framework for the relationship between somatotype and temperament is complex and sophisticated, a mixture of argument from physiology and argument from analogy. For example, he suggests that the endomorph's basal metabolism, pulse, breathing rate and temperature are all often slower and lower than average; hence their tendency to laziness and relaxation. Beyond this, however, he conceptualizes the type as 'biologically introverted', with all the energy pulled in towards the abdomen (which also describes parasympathetic dominance in the autonomic nervous system); and he argues that endomorphs balance this biological introversion by being psychologically extraverted. In a different metaphor, he suggests that they assimilate people and relationships in a parallel way to their assimilation of food. These explanatory models are similar in spirit to those of Reich and his followers, although different in detail (see Chapter 3).

Sheldon's ideas have never been rebutted, but they are now generally seen as dated and old-fashioned rather than false. Perhaps this is because no-one has quite found a way to develop them further, although recent developments in neuroscience might offer ways to do this. O'Hanrahan (1999) relates Sheldon's somatotypes to the nine Enneagram types (see Chapter 6), and suggests appropriate counselling and body psychotherapy strategies for approaching each type (see Table 5.6).

Predisposition to illness

A good deal of research has been done to suggest that particular personality types are prone to develop particular illnesses, and some of this has filtered through into therapy and counselling. The material has been brought together by Joan Arehart-Treichel (1981) as a description of six 'biotypes', as shown in Table 5.7. (She also includes a seventh, or 'mental disorder', type.)

Virtually all of Arehart-Treichel's biotypes seem to share both a tendency to repress 'negative' emotions like grief and anger, and a tendency to experience sexual difficulties: a striking endorsement of the theories of Reich and other humanistic therapists. (In fact, the gastrointestinal type, in particular, seems a close match for Reich's version of the anal character, whom he suggests will be prone to intestinal illness.)

Table 5.7   (based on Arehart-Treichel 1981)

	Early life experience	*Psychological traits*
Cancer	Trauma; lack of love	Repressed, self-blaming, negative, compliant, apparently well-adjusted and stable
Heart attack	Close to parents; encouraged to achieve	Ambitious, hard-working, competitive, stressed, angry
Gastrointestinal	Trauma; over-dependence	Repressed, compulsive caring, perfectionist
Allergy	Dominating mother/ ineffectual father	Repressed hostility, conscientious, obsessive
Rheumatoid arthritis	One harsh and rejecting parent; often broken home	Hypersensitive, dependence masked by dominating behaviour
Headache	Strict upbringing	Punitive conscience

Personality tests

A number of practitioners, particularly in the United States, are drawn to the use of diagnostic tests (Cronbach 1990), some of which claim to measure how an individual fits into one or another system of personality types. Two examples already discussed in Chapter 4 are the Myers-Briggs and the Gray-Wheelwrights inventories; a third is the Minnesota Multiphasic Personality Inventory (MMPI). It is important to grasp two points about these type of tests. First, by their nature they assume a particular set of categories – a particular typology of personality that is built into their initial structure. Secondly, unlike the Jungian inventories, the MMPI is *empirically keyed*; in other words, instead of asking questions that common sense would judge to be relevant to the qualities being measured ('face validity'), it asks questions that have been empirically shown to correlate with the relevant qualities. For example, to establish a scale for depression, the MMPI authors tested both depressed patients and controls, and included in the final inventory whatever questions distinguished depressed from non-depressed individuals, regardless of their apparent link with depression (Cook 1984: 16).

The use of the word 'patients' in the last sentence indicates the key limitation of the MMPI. The test sets out to measure nine categories – hypochondria, depression, hysteria, psychopathy, paranoia, psychasthenia, schizophrenia, mania, and placing on a masculinity–femininity scale. It relies completely on *psychiatric diagnoses* of these nine states to establish its original correlations. Hence its measurements are precisely as good as the initial diagnoses – it simply replicates the clinical judgement of the psychiatrists involved. Measures like the MMPI are time-saving, rather than offering any increase in accuracy and they offer much less by way of insight. And, of course, they rely on predetermined categories, a personality typology that is built into the system. In a different way, the same is true of the California Personality Inventory (CPI), 'the sane person's MMPI' as it is sometimes known. It uses a set of 'folk-psychology' categories like sociability, submissiveness, and so on. The questions are constructed to correlate with how the original participants were rated on these qualities by other people.

There is nothing wrong with therapists using personality inventories if they choose to – but they need to be clear that they are in effect submitting their own clinical judgement not to some sort of objective scientific construct, but to the entirely human judgement of those clinicians who were used to construct the inventory. (These tools have, of course, been repeatedly calibrated, and may be said to represent the collective wisdom of many clinicians.) They also need to be clear that all such inventories have a specific theory of personality built into them, and will necessarily replicate that theory in their results.

Conclusion

It will be apparent that the emphasis of humanistic therapies on individual uniqueness, and their suspicion of intellectual systems, has biased them against personality typologies. A superficial exploration might even conclude that there are no such typologies in humanistic approaches. Looking in more depth, however, we can find a good deal of relevant material, and conclude that perhaps every approach except person-centred therapy at least allows for, if not encourages, the use of typological structures.

These particular systems have, however, a strong tendency to be *ad hoc*, off-the-peg, over-empirical or borrowed from other disciplines, or various combinations of these. Although they are often interesting and thought-stimulating, nothing like the same amount of hard thinking has gone into them as has been invested in the psychodynamic systems of character and personality types. There is more work here crying out to be done; and perhaps some of the transpersonal systems that we consider in the next chapter could make a useful contribution.

C H A P T E R **6**

Transpersonal typologies

Many approaches that can broadly be termed 'transpersonal' have systems for understanding personality. What these all, perhaps, have in common is that they connect or relate the individual personality to something beyond the material and the social, something which is often termed 'spirit'. Transpersonal therapies have often adopted systems that are not psychotherapeutic in origin; for example, astrology and the Tarot have both been used for many centuries as modes of fortune-telling. Their applicability to therapy perhaps sheds some interesting light on the real nature of fortune-telling; in fact, many practitioners would claim that astrology and the Tarot both actually originated as psychological disciplines.

As we continue, it will be noticeable that many of the systems we look at draw on Jungian theory and, in turn, sometimes feed back into that theory, as for example Mary Loomis (1991) draws on the Medicine Wheel system for her development of new Jungian ideas (see Chapter 4). Jung is often regarded as giving psychological respectability to esoteric and 'New Age' ideas; oddly, perhaps, given his own strong privileging of high Western culture. Jung is certainly interested in the whole range of esoteric approaches, but most of these, with the partial exception of alchemy (Jung [1953] 1969), he treats as misapprehensions of genuine psychological data (Jung [1958] 1970, 1962). In turn, a good deal of the application of Jungian ideas to esoteric personality systems is itself based on simplification and misunderstanding.

The four elements

Both astrology and the Tarot, together with some others, are founded
on the pattern of the four elements, a very ancient component of
Western thought documented as far back as ancient Egypt and Greece
(Gullan-Whurr 1987). This system can be used as a template for
grasping a number of approaches that either are directly based upon
it or employ closely parallel concepts from other cultures. In the
West, as in the East, the elements are several things at once: they are
basic building blocks both of matter and of the psyche, along the
lines of the alchemical saying 'As above, so below' – in other words,
the macrocosmic universe is mirrored in the microcosm of the human mind (Burland 1967; Fabricius 1994). Different world traditions
identify different numbers of elements, and assign to them somewhat different qualities, as we shall see; but in the Western tradition, the four elements are known as Earth, Air, Fire and Water, and
frequently displayed as a cross within a circle (Fig. 6.1).

A great deal could be said about Fig. 6.1, but for our purposes two
things are especially important. First, it shows each element as
composed from a combination of two qualities: fire is hot and dry,
water is cool and moist, and so on. The diagram also asserts that air
is hot and moist, something that makes a lot more sense in the
Eastern Mediterranean where it originated than it does in Britain, for

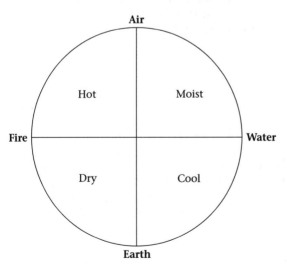

Figure 6.1

example! This illustrates the important general principle that systems of this kind, which synthesize different sorts of qualities into a single form, tend strongly to be *local* in structure.

The elements can be identified with many and various qualities of the world, including directions, colours, physical states (i.e. solid, liquid, gas and plasma), weather, seasons, astronomical phenomena, animals, plants, as well as with specifically human qualities and functions. Hence they offer many possibilities of identifying correspondences between different levels and layers of reality, and of creating richly concrete expressions of psychological tendencies. However, many of these features and their correspondence are meaningful in a particular culture or geographical location, rather than universally. As a simple example, which of the four directions corresponds to Water will rather depend on which way the ocean is from where I live. In a similar way, the 'meaning' of items like colour is completely culturally defined; in China, for example, white is the colour of mourning.

The other feature to notice is that the diagram organizes the elements into *pairs*, which represent polarities within the basic set of four: fire and water, earth and air, are each seen as polar oppositions that interact with each other. In terms of human psychological qualities, these paired polarities are often understood as gendered, with fire and air seen as 'masculine' and water and earth as 'feminine'. And the elements are identified with traditionally gendered faculties or qualities: earth with physical sensation and activity, water with emotion and sympathy, fire with will and action, and air with thinking and decision. As in Eastern systems, this gendering clearly implies a particular set of what are ultimately political notions about what qualities are appropriate for men and for women – even when the standard disclaimer is made that masculinity and femininity appear in both genders.

If working through the chapters of this book in sequence, the reader will have noticed a considerable parallel between the system of the four elements, as laid out in simple terms here, and Jung's typology of four functions. The parallel is no coincidence: Jung deliberately based his typology on the traditional four-element pattern, which he regarded as an archetypal reality of the human psyche: 'Jung devoted practically the whole of his life's work to demonstrating the vast psychological significance of the number four' (von Franz 1974: 115). The four elements had already given rise to the ancient and mediaeval system of physical humours and psychological temperaments, as shown in Table 6.1.

Table 6.1 (based on Gullan-Whurr 1987)

	Earth	*Air*	*Fire*	*Water*
Humour	Black bile	Blood	Yellow bile	Phlegm
Temperament	Melancholic	Sanguine	Choleric	Phlegmatic
Traits	Slow, passive, suspicious	Subtle, penetrating, easily bored	Honest, dynamic, argumentative	Sensitive, impressionable

In a similar way to traditional Chinese medicine – although with less documented effectiveness of treatment – Western elemental theory essentially conflates the physical and the psychological into a single holistic system. A person who is ruled by the element of Air, for example, will have a physiognomy that expresses airy qualities, like a fresh and rosy complexion (if they are white); and a constitution in which the blood plays a principal role, although just as with Chinese medicine, 'blood' here cannot be simply identified with the red fluid in our veins and arteries. Such a person will have a personality of a sanguine nature, tending to be quick-witted, energetic, curious and optimistic. (For a modern account of the system of temperaments as taught by Rudolf Steiner, see Wilkinson 1967.)

Astrology

Although there is no reason why the traditional temperaments could not be applied directly to psychotherapy, few therapists have yet done so. However, astrology, which derives in large part from the four-element system, has been quite widely used in psychotherapy and counselling since its modern recasting as a psychologically oriented discipline (Rudhyar 1972; Arroyo 1975; Greene 1977; Schermer 1989). Although astrology involves several components that interact in complex ways, the four elements are a crucial factor: each of the twelve zodiacal signs is assigned to one of the elements, and in drawing up an individual chart one of the factors that an astrologer immediately looks for is the balance of elements – how many of the planets or significant points appear in signs ruled by each element, whether any of the elements is unrepresented, and so on. This gives key information about the individual's overall style of personality.

Similarly, the Tarot, which is also used in counselling and psycho-therapy (although somewhat less widely than astrology), is also structured through the four-element system: each of the four tarot suits of Coins, Swords, Cups and Wands corresponds to one of the elements, Earth, Air, Water and Fire respectively (Gardner 1974). Although the Tarot has mainly been a tool for predicting future events, it can also be used, like a natal horoscope, to define the pattern of an individual's personality – their strengths and weaknesses, creative and destructive factors, potential for growth and for stagnation – as a basis for therapeutic work (Gardner 1970, 1974; Nichols 1984).

Most therapeutic applications of astrology and the Tarot draw the bulk of their inspiration from Jung. In fact, there is a circle of influence here: as we have observed above, Jung drew on the four-element system for his own theories and, in turn, others have interpreted the four elements, and astrology and the tarot in general, in Jungian terms (Greene 1977; Nichols 1984). Liz Greene, a Jungian analyst and one of the foremost exponents of astrological counselling, heads the Centre for Psychological Astrology in London, which offers 'a unique workshop and professional training programme designed to foster the cross fertilisation of the fields of astrology and depth, humanistic and transpersonal psychology' (Centre for Psychological Astrology 2000). The objectives of this training are:

> To provide students with a solid and broad base of knowledge both within the realm of traditional astrological symbolism and technique in the field of psychology, so that the astrological chart can be sensitively understood and interpreted in the light of modern psychological thought . . .
>
> To make available to students psychologically qualified case supervision along with background seminars in counselling skills and techniques which would raise the standard and effectiveness of astrological consultation . . .
>
> To encourage investigation and research into the links between astrology, psychological models and therapeutic techniques.
>
> (Centre for Psychological Astrology 2000)

There are parallel programmes in the USA and Europe.

The Medicine Wheel

The Medicine Wheel system (Storm 1972; Bopp *et al.* 1984), derives mainly from Native American tribes of the Great Plains, but with

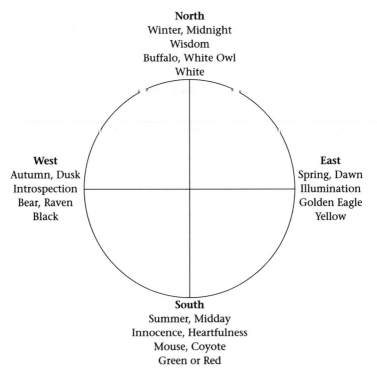

North
Winter, Midnight
Wisdom
Buffalo, White Owl
White

West
Autumn, Dusk
Introspection
Bear, Raven
Black

East
Spring, Dawn
Illumination
Golden Eagle
Yellow

South
Summer, Midday
Innocence, Heartfulness
Mouse, Coyote
Green or Red

Figure 6.2   (based on Storm 1972; Medicine Eagle 1991)

parallels throughout Amerindian cultures. It is in some ways uncannily similar to the four elements approach. Like the four elements, its essence can be expressed through the image of a cross within a circle; it is founded on the identity of macrocosm and microcosm; and it is made up of a series of correspondences between different features and levels of reality, including human psychology (see Fig. 6.2). All the specific details of these correspondences, however, are different between the two systems, as is true of other parallel systems around the world.

The parallels between the Western and Native American systems are so great, in fact, that a Medicine Wheel astrology has been produced. Synthetic in both senses of the word, this draws heavily on the traditional Old World symbolism of the twelve zodiac signs, but uses North American animals to represent them (Sun Bear and Wabun 1980). This system is widely used for astrological counselling in the USA.

The Medicine Wheel system has great psychological subtlety, and both can be and is being used in psychotherapy and counselling as the basis for a system of personality types.

> All things of the Universe Wheel have spirit and life . . . But it is only man, of all the Beings on the Wheel, who is a determiner. Our determining spirit can be made whole only through the learning of our harmony with all our brothers and sisters, and with all the other spirits of the Universe. To do this we must learn to seek and perceive. We must do this to find our place within the Medicine Wheel.
>
> (Storm 1972: 5)

We have already referred in Chapter 4 to the use made of the Medicine Wheel in a Jungian context by Mary Loomis.

Ayurveda

Eastern civilizations have been using sophisticated psychological models of personality, and the equivalent of psychotherapeutic intervention, for thousands of years. In India, Ayurvedic parallels to psychiatry, psychology and psychotherapy are established traditions (Kingsland and Kingsland 1977; Hills 1977). Ayurveda is a holistic system for bodymind healing, which, like Western transpersonal approaches, emphasizes the spiritual aspect of each individual, the God within, alongside the personal soul and its embodiment. Just as we are all aspects of one God, so we are also composed from the same inner psychological, emotional and soul components. It is the individual and unique mixing of these components that creates our sense of individuality and personality type. The personality types are gathered together into groupings of similar traits or characteristics.

The Ayurvedic system is also based on an elemental pattern – but this time one of five elements (the Western four plus Ether), which are combined with a three-fold pattern, equivalent to the humours and temperaments, to create eight personality types. The process of creation starts with The One, then splits into a duality seen as masculine and feminine, Purusha and Prakritti, the Sun and the Moon. It is the intermingling of these two elements that is said to give rise to the five elements and the eight personality types.

The three basic Ayurvedic temperaments, or gunas ('cords'), which correspond to physical qualities known as doshas, are as follows:

- *Sattva* (Sanskrit root word *Sat*, the radiance of being) is the quality of clear, pure intellect. Sattva dominated personalities tend towards the academic, are intellectual and not ruled by emotion.
- *Rajas* (Sanskrit root word *Raj*, to glow red with energy) is the quality of movement and energy. Rajas dominated personalities tend towards energetic activities and are in touch with their emotions.
- *Tamas* (Sanskrit root word *Tam*, to perish or to become sad) is the quality of inertia or weight. Tamas dominated personalities tend to be either fixed and immovable, or in motion and unstoppable.

The seven chakra personality types

Although individuals may be described simply as guna types, the gunas form the basic building blocks of a more elaborate, seven-fold personality model called the chakra system. The Ayurvedic psychologist is seeking to identify the chakra type and to enable the client to create a balance that will allow them equal access to all three guna qualities, which, in turn, will enable them to become self-healing.

A chakra ('wheel' in Sanskrit) is described as an energy vortex in the field or aura surrounding the physical body (Hills 1977). There are seven chakras, each situated over a nerve complex and related to an endocrine gland; different personality types have different chakra configurations of varying brightness and intensity. Each chakra type has an attachment to the need for security peculiar to that chakra, and this governs their personality, behaviour and responses (Kingsland 1973).

In the following section – drawing on Hills (1977) and Kingsland and Kingsland (1977) – the guna qualities of each personality type are shown by the letters s or S, r or R and t or T, following the name of the chakra in the heading. Gunas which are *strong* in this type are indicated by the *capital* letter, and gunas which are *weak* by the *lower-case* letter (see also Table 6.2).

1 *Muladhara* (srT). Over the gonads in the coccygial nervous plexus. Lacking the insight of Sattva and the emotional attachment of Rajas, this personality becomes behaviourally dominated. Attracted to transient external stimuli, impelled to the manipulation of objects around them, and unaware of the inner worlds of others, they tend to express energy through sexual, physical or sporting activity. Often a loner, lacking social graces, seeking to conquer opposite sex, expecting action from others on demand.

2 *Svadisthana* (sRt). Over the lower abdomen in the sacral nervous plexus, related to the adrenal glands. Emotionally dominated by Rajas, they are unrealistically optimistic, tending to look to the future rather than the 'now'. Personal identity is built on being part of a group, leading to a strong sense of 'us' and 'them' with all the associated prejudices and hostilities. More sensual than sexual, the group tends to reinforce belonging with stroking and touching.

3 *Manipura* (Srt). Related to the pancreas and sited over the solar plexus in the lumbar nervous plexus. A personality with the butterfly energy of the Sattva intellect, but without the grounding to support their life stance. Intellectually and academically bright, needing to analyse everything, seeking mental excitement and novelty, although unable to maintain committed relationships: easily bored and stifled by routine.

4 *Anhatta* (sRT). Related to the thymus and sited over the heart in the brachial nervous plexus. A desire for power and recognition unregulated by reason. This type is often found in business people, where apparent confidence camouflages self-doubt. An insecure drive towards power and recognition can lead to strong feelings of jealousy and possessiveness.

5 *Vishuddha* (SrT). Related to the thyroid and para-thyroids and sited over the cervical nervous plexus. A lack of emotional connection to the present can manifest as refusing personal responsibility for one's actions. Controlled by tradition, this dutiful personality seeks to dominate inferiors and defers to superiors. Tends to be stuck in fixed opinions and ideas. Conflicts between the need for safe contentment and the discontent of stagnation can lead to episodes of apparent uncharacteristic or outrageous behaviour.

6 *Ajna* (SRt). Related to the pituitary and sited over the centre of the forehead at the 'third eye'. Inability to act on thoughts and feeling leads this personality type to take an inward path of meditation, contemplation and prayer. Often feeling powerless to affect the worldly events, Ajna types gather together in ashram or monastic type settings where they can live a quiet harmonious life surrounded by others with a similar depth of feeling.

7 *Sahasra* (SRT). Towards the top of the skull above and behind the pituitary gland, and related to the pineal. This type has reached a state of guna balance, the forerunner of enlightenment. The personality is able to identify problems, and has the commitment and weight to follow through a course of action to completion.

Table 6.2 (based on Kingsland and Kingsland 1977; Hills 1977)

Chakra name	Endocrine gland	Colour	Personality conflict	Drive	Appropriate yoga
Withdrawn (no chakra)	None	Magenta	Fantasy vs reality	Avoidance	None
Sahasra	Pineal	Violet	Creating heaven/hell	Creative problem-solving	Tantra
Ajna	Pituitary	Indigo	Compassion vs powerlessness	Peace and harmony	Raja
Vishuddha	Thyroid and parathyroid	Blue	Thinking vs feeling; comfort vs activity	Structure, organization, status quo	Mantra
Anhatta	Thymus	Green	Need for recognition vs limitations of jealousy and selfishness	Emotional power of recognition	Bhakti
Manipura	Pancreas	Yellow	Drive for change vs emptiness of impermanence	Intellectual self-expression	Gnani
Svadisthana	Adrenal	Orange	Personal responsibility vs group identity	Social and sensual	Hatha
Muladhara	Gonads	Red	Thinking vs feeling; influencing others vs being left alone	Physical and sexual	Karma

This is the stage of the problem-solver, the creative genius; but those with the creative power to inspire others must choose between creating heaven or hell.

8 *Fantastical withdrawn personality type* (srt). No bodily site. The personality is lost and withdrawn from the world living in an inner construct of fantasy that is usually, although not always, warm and safe. Interaction with this personality type is difficult; it can seem as though they are at the other end of a long tube, and often quite unaware of the outside world.

Ayurvedic psychotherapy

Just as modern Reichians would say about the character positions, all the chakra types described above are within each of us. However, most people will identify with one chakra area and use it as their basic personality building block. As someone develops, they will gain greater access to the different chakras. Although the final goal of Ayurvedic psychotherapy is the transcendence of the personality through enlightenment, the short-term therapeutic goal is to enable the person to access the seventh chakra, the Sahasra, where problem-solving can begin. It has been said that people lacking access to the Sahasra describe their problems, while those accessing the Sahasra describe what they are doing about their problems!

Development of the relationship between the individual personality and the creative force is seen by Ayurvedic therapy as the ultimate purpose of life. There is a universal and natural state of spiritual, mental, emotional and physical equilibrium within all things. Life is understood to be an ongoing learning process carried on through many incarnations, as the personality or soul moves from one body, evolving all the time. The individual who has achieved total balance has achieved a state of grace usually termed 'enlightenment' (Mishra 1959; Hills 1968; Kingsland and Kingsland 1976, 1977). It is the state of imbalance that is the essence of each personality type (Hills 1968). This suggests that in creating, re-creating or even changing the current state of balance of the individual, it is possible to change the essential personality of that person and, finally, to reach a state of enlightenment that is beyond personality: this is often described as 'self-annihilation'. Psychotherapy in this context is an enabling of this process.

Although in Western models of personality types the individual personality is often seen as fixed, or becoming fixed at an early stage of childhood – so that at best the individual may be expected to change marginally throughout their lifetime through a process of maturation and problem-solving – Ayurveda and other Eastern models describe a process of continual change. The personality archetypes are seen as way stations in an evolutionary journey from the base ignorance of unconsciousness or deep asleep-ness to enlightenment or awake-ness (Hills 1968; Kingsland and Kingsland 1976; MacCuish *et al.* 1998). Each station is a stage of personality development and a place to linger, ultimately learn and then move on. The stay might be a few minutes or years or several lifetimes. Each individual's growth is valued as an aspect of the entire universe's evolutionary process.

Yoga, often seen in the West as a series of keep-fit exercises, is in Ayurvedic terms composed of specific bodymind tools for therapeutic interventions with different personality types. For each personality type, an individual Yoga or way of being has been developed to help each personality archetype to overcome their inhibitions to enlightenment. Hatha Yoga, as an ancient Ayurvedic science, has a precise aetiological and nosological model of body tension as an expression of both personality archetype and psychological problems. Based around the chakra system, the model is as follows:

- *Physical identity or conflict*: tension in the area of the coccyx and buttocks, anal, bowel and sexual problems.
- *Social identity or conflict*: tension in the lower back and back of legs, renal and adrenal problems.
- *Intellectual identity or conflict*: tension in the solar plexus and front of legs, pancreatic and dermatological problems.
- *Emotional identity or conflict*: tension in the chest, ribs and sternum, cardiovascular and respiratory problems.
- *Mental identity or conflict*: tension in the shoulders, neck and throat, thyroid and parathyroid problems.
- *Intuitive identity or conflict*: tension in the face, headaches and pituitary problems.
- *Creative identity or conflict*: tension in the scalp, brain and central nervous system problems.

Ken Wilber

One of the best known figures in transpersonal psychology is Ken Wilber, who through a number of long books (e.g. Wilber 1995,

1996) has achieved a vast synthesis of psychological systems from around the world, notably Hindu (including Ayurvedic) and Buddhist, as well as many Western approaches. Wilber seeks to reinstate the nineteenth-century concept of the Perennial Philosophy, a universal spiritual wisdom that expresses itself in many forms. As he puts it, the Perennial Philosophy combines ontogeny and phylogeny; in other words, there is an intrinsically progressive developmental path to be traversed both by each human being and by the human race as a whole, a path which, in traditional terms, takes us from 'matter' to 'spirit'.

The immediate relevance of all this for our purpose is that Wilber defines a number of stages (the exact number varies, but in his 1996 book he gives eight) along this path – stages that can be aligned with the position of any individual person, and thus used as a psycho-taxonomy. His system has been hailed by some psychotherapists (e.g. Rowan 1993, 1996) because it offers a way of integrating the spiritual into therapy, through Wilber's concept of the 'Centaur' level. At this level, 'mind and body, after being clearly differentiated, are brought into a higher-order integration' (Wilber 1996: 339), and what one may call 'enlightenment' starts to become the primary focus of energy.

Wilber's work has been ferociously attacked by the well-known humanistic theorist John Heron, for what Heron (1998: 82) terms his 'false hegemonic claims . . . that [his system] is perennial and preordained for the whole of mankind'. Specifically, Heron argues that Wilber's approach is 'gender-laden', in that the masculine is aligned with the spiritual and the feminine with the material, while spirit is 'always on a higher level' (p. 77); and that despite paying lip-service to a non-hierarchical understanding, the material, and the level of individual existence, are regarded by Wilber as essentially illusions to be transcended within a reductive unity (Heron 1992: 197ff.).

Feeling and personhood

Heron (1992) has his own project for a unified psychology of mind, body and spirit, laid out in his book *Feeling and Personhood*, which can also be used as the basis for a psycho-taxonomy. However, like several other writers, Heron warns that he is describing stages or moments of the individual personality more than distinct types, and even then he warns against taking these stages as sequential rather than interwoven and often simultaneous (pp. 52–3). Heron identifies eight 'states of personhood', the first four of which he argues are in a sense 'prepersonal' – 'they comprise the loam, the ground, the humus out of which the top four grow'. In contradistinction to Wilber, Heron is concerned to avoid any implication of transcendence: his entire system is constructed from 'up hierarchies', where the 'higher' is dependent on the 'lower'.

The first four, prepersonal states, then, are the 'primal', a state of foetal fusion with the world; the 'spontaneous', or the playing child; the 'compulsive', or wounded child; and the 'conventional', or socialized and languaged individual. These four, according to Heron (1992: 54–8), will reliably appear in this developmental sequence. The second four, which may not appear in this order, are the 'creative', or inner-directed; the 'self-creating', a state where a person is consciously committed to their own growth; the 'self-transfiguring', where they are in the process of realizing spiritual and psychic potential; and the 'charismatic', a state when someone 'marries spirit, subtle and gross matter in a seamless radiating whole' (Heron 1992: 58–63).

The Enneagram

Although now used by many counsellors and psychotherapists, the Enneagram as a system of personality types derives from the spiritual teachings of G.I. Gurdjieff (J. Webb 1980; Bennett 1983). The Enneagram itself is a diagram of nine points within a circle, with specific patterns of connections between those points (see Fig. 6.3). The nine points can be used to categorize a number of different aspects of human beings – emotions, virtues and vices, and other types of quality – but for our purposes the relevant Enneagram is that of personality. The types described are regarded as 'normal and high-functioning people, rather than pathological trends' (Palmer 1991: 233); a person adopts their type 'to protect a specific aspect of our essence (higher, or divine, self) which was particularly vulnerable in the infant' (K. Webb 1996: 3). The arrows between types show how each type will change under stress, and also allows description of the interactions between types.

There is a great deal of literature on these nine types, but they are briefly described in Table 6.3. As can be seen, the Enneagram system has a strong moral flavour to it, with a good deal of emphasis on self-improvement. The Enneagram is used in spiritual development

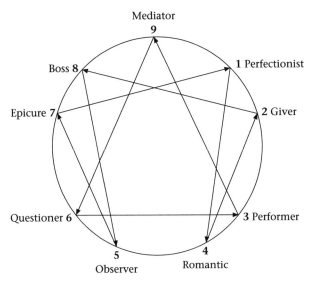

Figure 6.3 (based on Webb 1996)

(Rohr 1990; Zuercher 1992), notably as a key element in Oscar Ichazo's Arica Institute (Lilly 1973). It is also widely used as a counselling and self-improvement tool (Palmer 1991, 1994; K. Webb 1996).

Archetypal systems

Our final group of typologies are all based on Jung's concept of the archetype, or personified psychic essence. Each one describes human beings in terms of their approximation to the embodiment of specific sets of archetypes; in the case of the first three systems, sets which are identified with the Greek goddesses. (As Jung sees it, gods and goddesses from any culture are themselves representations of archetypes that have an objective existence within the human psyche.)

Drawing on the seminal work of Nor Hall (1980) in developing a Jungian psychology of the feminine, Jean Shineda Bolen (1984) offers a systematic correlation of female personality types based on seven major Greek goddesses, divided into three groups, as in Table 6.4: 'virgin goddesses' representing women's independent, self-sufficient qualities; 'vulnerable goddesses' representing women's need for bonding and relationship; and a single 'alchemical goddess', motivating women to transform and develop. These goddesses also

Table 6.3 (based on Palmer 1994; Webb 1996)

	Description	'Passion'	Weakness
1 Perfectionist	Critical of self and others; finds it hard to relax and enjoy; good organizer	Anger	Resentment
2 Giver	Active, generous, optimistic; compulsive carer who ignores own needs	Pride	Flattery
3 Performer	High energy workaholic; competitive, success-oriented, good leader; out of touch with feelings	Self-deception	Vanity
4 Romantic	Artistic, passionate, empathic, feeling-centred; searching for meaning and for partnership	Envy	Melancholy
5 Observer	Detached and objective; very private, needing solitude; compartmentalized; intellectual	Avarice	Stinginess
6 Questioner	Anxious and suspicious of life; dislikes and questions authority	Fear	Cowardice
7 Epicure	Charming and elusive, 'Peter Pan' type who excludes unpleasantness	Gluttony	Obsessive planning
8 Boss	Assertive, all-or-nothing approach; either a leader or rugged individualist; fighter for justice	Lust for life	Vengeance
9 Mediator	Peacemaker who understands everyone's point of view (except their own); busy but procrastinating	Sloth	Indolence

Table 6.4 (based on Bolen 1984)

Group	Goddess	Role
Virgin goddesses	Artemis	Sister, competitor, feminist
	Athena	Father's daughter, strategist
	Hestia	Maiden aunt, wise woman
Vulnerable goddesses	Hera	Wife, commitment maker
	Demeter	Mother, nurturer
	Persephone	Mother's daughter, receptive
Alchemical goddess	Aphrodite	Lover, creative woman

Table 6.5 (based on Woolger and Woolger 1989)

	Independence	*Power*	*Love*
Extraverted	Athena (civilization)	Hera (rulership)	Aphrodite (eros)
Introverted	Artemis (nature)	Persephone (underworld)	Demeter (mother)

represent different family roles open to women. Bolen (1984: 10) suggests that the goddess archetypes offer an explanation for 'inconsistencies between women's behavior and Jung's theory of psychological types' – notably, the failure to fit into 'either/or' structures noted by Singer and Loomis (1984) [see also Loomis (1991) and Singer (1995) in Chapter 4]:

> As a woman 'shifts gears' and goes from one facet of herself to another, she can shift from one goddess pattern to another ... This shifting explains the difficulty that a many-sided woman has determining what Jungian type she is ... The prevailing 'goddess' explains how one function ... can paradoxically be both highly developed and unconscious.
>
> (Bolen 1984: 10–11)

Bolen also points out the dangers of what Jung terms 'inflation', which is the overwhelming of the ego by an archetype, in this case causing psychiatric symptoms parallel to the goddess's attributes.

Jennifer and Roger Woolger (1989) have developed an alternative structuring of similar Jungian and mythological material (Table 6.5);

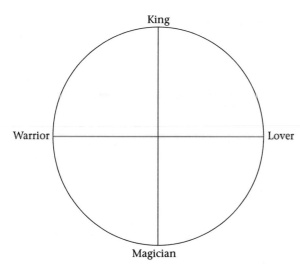

Figure 6.4 (based on Moore and Gillette 1990)

for whatever reason, they choose to omit the goddess Hestia, who in Bolen's scheme represents the unmarried older woman – possibly because their goddess archetypes are those 'that strike us as the most active in the lives of modern women and in contemporary society' (Woolger and Woolger 1994: 116). Theirs is an interesting example of how social and cultural factors can weight a personality typology. They stress that 'unlike Sun-sign astrology, in which one is fixed as a Pisces or a Leo, every woman is a complex mixture of all the goddess types' (Woolger and Woolger 1989: 118).

Bolen (1989) has also written about *The Gods in Every Man*; and another archetypal system for men is that constructed within the Men's Movement in the United States by Moore and Gillette (1990). Moore and Gillette, again consciously echoing Jung, suggest a 'quaternio' of four masculine archetypes, grouped into two polar pairs (see Fig. 6.4). In this system, the King is seen as the primal and most important of the four archetypes, which, when it is functioning well, includes the others within itself – the good King is also a good Magician, Warrior and Lover. Each of the four also has an immature version – the Divine Child, Hero, Precocious Child and Oedipal Child, respectively. Moore and Gillette indicate creative and harmful ways in which each of these archetypal energies can express itself, and suggest that any attempt to simply suppress an archetype – for instance, to eliminate the Warrior energy in men – will succeed

Table 6.6 (based on Moore and Gillette 1990)

	Creative expression	*Active shadow*	*Passive shadow*
King	'God in his masculine form within every man'; father, head of family; centredness	The tyrant: authoritarianism, power over others, domination	The weakling: absence of authority and power
Warrior	Skill, discipline and control in the service of transpersonal loyalties	The sadist: destructiveness, violence, hard-heartedness	The masochist: embracing of violence and pain
Magician	Knowledge, mastery, initiation; 'the observing ego'	The detached manipulator: techno-fix, control	The denying 'innocent: abandoning responsibility, embracing helplessness
Lover	Empathy; joy in and commitment to life; passion	The addicted lover: indulgence, greed	The impotent lover: over-sensitivity,

only in creating its harmful expression, or 'shadow', in either a 'positive' (overcharged) or 'negative' (underpowered) form (see Table 6.6). They suggest that the different archetypes need to be balanced by each other for their best expression.

As may already be apparent, Moore and Gillette are vulnerable to criticism both for sexism (privileging masculine elements and, in-deed, a particularly and uncritically traditional set of such elements) and for essentialism (belief in an intrinsic and absolute difference between male and female psychologies). The same criticism of essent-ialism can be made against both Bolen (1989) and the Woolgers (1994). This accurately reflects a quality of Jung's archetypal theory (Wehr 1987; Young-Eisendrath and Wiedemann 1987).

Conclusion

It has been hard in this chapter to avoid the appearance of simply mounting a procession of one system after another. Certainly, we have described a plethora of personality types, which cannot all be reduced to recensions of the same basic theory. What does link these different systems is their emphasis on the transpersonal at each person's core, whether expressed as the spiritual, God, the Ultimate or otherwise. As Webb puts it in describing the Enneagram, 'the unique and heartening aspect of the Enneagram theory is that our "false" personality reflects, as in a mirror image, our highest self' (K. Webb 1996: 3). She is mistaken, however, about the uniqueness of that particular typology. In fact, this is a theme common to many, indeed perhaps to most, theories of character and personality type. And it is to the question of what therapeutically useful similarities may exist between different theories of character and typology that we turn in our concluding chapter.

CHAPTER 7

Conclusion

The reader who has worked consecutively through the book to this point is, we presume, favourable to the use of personality typing in psychotherapy and counselling. However, they may well by this point feel more than replete with the number and variety of systems that are available for such use. One relevant question, as we conclude this description of a conceptual set of approaches to understanding people and their behaviours, is whether there is any way constructively to narrow down the field of choice. For example, might it be possible to eliminate some of the options or, alternatively, to select some of them as being the most relevant? Furthermore, is there any scope for synthesis and integration, which might lead to the emergence of one or two meta-systems out of the profusion of existing approaches?

Choosing between systems

One immediately obvious point is that many, if not all, of the typologies we have described are conceptually anchored in a specific approach to therapy; in other words, which typology therapists use depends to a great extent on the form of psychotherapy they are practising. It is hard to imagine someone using the categories of psychoanalytic character theory, for example, without also using the fundamental concepts of psychoanalytic therapy itself, and indeed its therapeutic structure and techniques. This is even more true of tightly defined approaches such as Ayurveda, the Enneagram and astrological counselling.

The implication of this is that therapists who choose a particular typology do so mainly because it is in accord with the overall therapeutic approach they have also chosen. Nevertheless, it is also true that many therapists and counsellors regard themselves either as *integrative*, looking for common elements across a range of approaches, or as *eclectic*, selecting what seems to them useful from that range, and perhaps allowing different systems to come into play in relation to different clients at different times. We will return to the question of integration; but is it possible to work eclectically with personality types? There seems no reason why it should not be, and this is in fact what the authors of this book often find themselves doing. One of us (N.T.) may think in a 'Reichian' way about one client's structure, and in a more 'Kleinian', 'Jungian' or even 'astrological' way about another (or in these alternative ways about the same client on different occasions). Even within his primary Reichian orientation, perhaps around 60 per cent of clients strongly indicate a particular character type; for working with the remaining 40 per cent, other tools, including other typologies, are helpful. The other author (M.J.) tends to stay more within Freudian, Kleinian and Object Relations approaches, but cannot fail (especially after working on this book) to be interested in associations to other typologies which occur at particular moments.

Practitioner diversity

This leads on to another sort of difference: as we have indicated already, an enormous variety of attitudes towards personality typing exist within as well as between the forms and sub-forms of therapy and counselling. For example, even though character theory in Reichian and post-Reichian thinking reaches perhaps its most highly developed expression and potentially has the most central role in that form of therapy, it is still easy to find practitioners who will readily acknowledge that they pay little or no attention to character, that it does not suit them, and that they find no place for it in their work. Within psychoanalysis, similarly, there are therapists who will state with confidence that the subject has fallen completely out of favour, and that this is something that analysts *used* to do; at the same time, other analysts are energetically publishing articles about character theory (see, for example, the debate on this question in Stein 1969; Schafer 1979). Equally, in therapies like Transactional Analysis, which pay comparatively little attention to typology, there is a minority of practitioners who take a strong and creative interest in the topic. In other words, it is very much a matter of individual predilection – perhaps related to personality type! – whether or not a practitioner focuses on the study of character and types; and also, at least to some extent, which typology he or she adopts. No-one has yet researched how this might correlate with differences, if any, in the practitioner's clinical work.

Integration

What, then, are the prospects for developing a synthesis of different typologies – or, failing that, at least a sort of Rosetta Stone, a meta-language for discussing points of contact and of difference between typologies? Despite the great variety of approaches, it does not take long to recognize that some perceptions of personality types are widely shared. Take, for instance, the set of correspondences in Table 7.1.

Some of these are plainly deliberate new versions or translations of each other – Reich's 'ocular' character is based on his research into the psychoanalytic schizoid category, and both Hakomi and Embodied-Relational Therapy rename the type (as well as developing some new conceptualizations of it) in the interests of increased clarity and value-neutrality. The same is true of Redecision Therapy, although working directly from the schizoid rather than the ocular type. The other references are, however, wholly or largely independent approaches, which arrive at a very similar description of one particular style of living and relating.

Table 7.1

Schizoid	Psychoanalysis
Ocular	Reich
Sensitive-analytic	Hakomi
Containing	Hakomi (new)
Boundary	Embodied-Relational
Introverted thinking	Jung
Desensitization/deflection	Gestalt
Creative daydreamer	Redecision
Extreme ectomorph	Sheldon
Fantastical withdrawn	Ayurveda
Observer	Enneagram

At the same time, even within the Reichian tradition, there are very significant differences of perception on the various character positions, as Chapter 3 makes clear. Some of these are possibly trivial, at least as viewed by an outside observer, but others are of theoretical importance. As an example, many American writers from Lowen (1958) onwards tend to downplay the 'hysteric' character or its equivalents, incorporating some of its traits into the 'psychopathic' position or renamed versions of it. Lowen (1976), followed by Keleman (1985), combine under the single label 'rigid' the traditional 'phallic' and 'hysteric' characters, which might well be seen as polar opposites, representing socially sanctioned masculine and feminine attitudes, respectively. Kurtz (1990) treats the traditional 'hysteric' character as simply childlike ('expressive/clinging'), and shifts its sexual and manipulative qualities to one sub-form of the psychopathic character ('charming/seductive'). Lowen also claims, against all other observers, that the anal character no longer manifests itself in the United States, being wholly a product of strict European toilet training! All of this could be described as a 'flight from the politicized pelvis' – an avoidance of issues of social control and its subversion which are deeply bound up with the concept of, in particular, the hysteric character (Totton and Edmondson 1988; Totton 1998).

If such meaningful differences exist within one fairly small branch of psychotherapy, how much the more so between quite distinct orientations? To return to Table 7.1, one important variation is that some of the type names carry with them a sense of pathology, or at least dysfunction; while others are value-neutral, or even positive in connotation. To be described as a schizoid character, or a fantastical withdrawn type, is a negative labelling, and creates a certain degree of disempowerment: the person so labelled is not being treated as a wholly responsible and functioning human being. The same does not apply to the label 'sensitive analytic' or 'introverted thinking type': such terms indicate a fruitful way of contacting and communicating with the person concerned; while on a deeper level they have some implications about what that person's relative strengths and weaknesses are likely to be.

This is one of the most fundamental differences among personality typologies, and one of the biggest hurdles to overcome before any real integration is possible: there is a fundamental difference between approaches that see character or personality as basically creative, a way of expressing our nature as human beings, and those that see it as basically problematic, a way of masking or limiting our nature as human beings. This difference of perception may in itself, once again, have some relevance to the personality of the perceiver.

Clearly, though, there is a point at which these two ways of viewing character, however opposed they are in some senses, actually meet. Character can be a vehicle both of expression *and* of limitation; in fact, Reichian theory would argue that this is exactly what character has to be, that its whole function is to protect people's capacity to express themselves – paradoxically through limiting that expression.

State and process

In teaching trainee therapists about the theory of character and personality types, the objection that one meets over and over again is that typology tries to 'fix' people – not in the sense of trying to mend them (although this argument is also made), but in the sense of not allowing for movement, for change and flow. For personality typing to find an integrated place within psychotherapy and counselling, this basic problem needs to be faced: that most typologies express themselves in a language of *states* and *entities*, which seems increasingly old-fashioned in the context of therapy that talks increasingly about *processes*. An integrative theory of character will need to redefine itself in this new language.

In doing so, we would argue that character theory can make a valuable contribution of its own, re-balancing a tendency within process theory towards a one-sided emphasis on change and flow. A new synthesis of the sort we are contemplating would treat state (or stasis) and process as inseparable and complementary concepts, each making sense of and delineating the other.

The complementarity of stasis and process can be seen throughout the natural world, particularly in living organisms, including human beings: organisms are goal-seeking adaptive systems, necessarily balancing stability with change (Wilden 1972). To put it simply, an organism which is all stability would be dead – metabolism implies change; but one which was all change would have no identity as an organism. Just as a cell needs a surrounding membrane to delineate the place where it is, human beings need 'edges' (Mindell 1985) – psychological boundaries that resist change – to delineate where they are; to exist at all. One can think of these edges as people's grip on their embodiment. In a strange way, fragments of a person have to be dead – unchanging – for them to live. Skin is an image of this paradox, of which Freud (1920) gives a very subtle account in *Beyond the Pleasure Principle* (see also Bick 1968; Houzel 1990).

Like *yin* and *yang*, process or stasis, if either is pushed to its extreme, will flip over into their complement. At this point the antithetical concepts of character and symptom, discussed in Chapter 2, become useful. We can think of symptoms as representing the limit point of fixed psychological states like character or personality type; while edges are the equivalent limit point of processes, the point at which change becomes stability. Symptoms are how stasis moves into process; edges are how process moves into stasis. If someone becomes too rigid and resistant to change, they tend to develop a symptom, an irritation, which destabilizes their boundary; conversely, if movement and change go too far and too fast, the same person will develop an edge, which stabilizes into a boundary.

These two events are different forms of feedback – *positive* and *negative*, respectively. 'Positive' and 'negative' here are, of course, not value judgements, but technical terms, referring to feedback that tends to amplify change (positive, as with electric guitars) or to damp it down (negative, as with thermostats). Almost throughout nature and in all mechanical systems, negative feedback predominates, tending towards stabilization and constancy (Wilden 1972). But much of what is characterized as 'process' – emergent properties, morphogenesis, change in general – is the result of positive feedback, tending towards growth; a tendency that also, in the long run, leads towards death. Positive and negative feedback – the phenomena of process and stasis – are both essential to living creatures, and also to social formations.

Such terminology is a somewhat out-dated way of talking about phenomena better described as 'dissipative structures' (Prigogine and Stengers 1985). Dissipative structures are phenomena that emerge spontaneously in 'far-from-equilibrium conditions'. Rather than the regular repetition of equilibrium-based systems, dissipative systems manifest uniqueness and specificity. In other words, they represent life: they are, precisely, forms of stasis emerging in the heart of process. Heraclitus pointed out that we cannot step in the 'same' river twice. However, the 'sameness' that does persist through the ongoing flow of water is one representation of a dissipative structure.

Returning to the psychological application of these ideas, we can state them generally as follows: to live we must die – not just at a singular moment, but continuously, dying into the future. At the same time, however, out of this continuous letting-go-to-change there emerges a continuity, a persistence of pattern that is complementary to change. A manifestation of this double movement is the play of polar tension between our drive to express ourselves and our drive to protect ourselves, which gives rise to double signals.

The concepts of traditional stasis-oriented psychology, looked at as complementary to process, take on a different look. In particular, it is possible to see many examples of stasis as far more creative and valuable than psychology has tended to think. 'Neurosis', 'character', and so on can be understood as attempts to re-balance the relationship of stasis and process in an individual's personality (often reflecting a need for re-balancing in the wider social field). The image of 're-balancing' itself combines stasis and process: a dynamic and temporary stability, as when we ride a bicycle, constantly shifting and swaying around a centre point, which, if we stuck to it rigidly, would cause us to fall.

Character is therefore a particularly rich and powerful concept, which has been rendered much less useful than it could be by its pathologization: a person's character position has too often been seen as simply a limitation or distortion, something that prevents them from changing and growing. This may sometimes or always be partially true; but character equally describes the particular style of growth and change taken by that individual. Just as a river needs its bed (and constantly changes the bed by its flow), so process needs a container or channel: a means of embodiment. An individual's character structure, the way in which their process expresses itself, needs the same sort of interested and friendly support as any other aspect of their being-in-the-world.

Of course, any container or channel can also be understood as a limitation. If we perform an action in one style, this means that we do not perform it in any number of other possible styles. This is more than just a logical postulate: character can throw up some very rigid limits, which a person can often benefit from challenging in themselves. But even the most rigid limits may most usefully be understood as moves in the game of being – as eccentric, 'characterful' ways of being someone. After all, process is also very capable of being 'destructive', 'eccentric', 'bizarre', 'irrational': both process and stasis can be inconvenient for their environment and, therefore, come under attack. In a political context, for example, there are some characterological qualities like stubbornness, persistence or demandingness that can be crucially important.

Just as we cannot assert *a priori* whether change or stability – radical or conservative, process or stasis – is the 'better' option in a

particular personal or political situation, so no valid choice can be
made between stasis and process in life as a whole: life depends on
the presence of both. The balance can shift between the two, but
people cannot choose one and not the other – not so long as they
want to stay embodied. Practitioners, then, need to be aware of and
to support and celebrate both poles of being in their clients or
patients – either of which can be primary or secondary in a particular moment: process, with its urge to change and flow, and stasis,
with its capacity to persist and survive.

Form and causation

Some version of these ideas, we suggest, is needed to inform an
integrative theory of personality types. And such ideas would naturally offer a way of conceptualizing the types themselves, as differential relationships or balances between stasis and process within
each individual. This could equally well be described as differential
attitudes in each individual *towards* stasis and process: a range between people who embrace stasis and fear process (psychological
conservatives), and those who embrace process and fear stasis (psychological radicals).

However, there still remains to be dealt with what is perhaps the
biggest and most general distinction within typologies: that which
revolves around the issue of *causation*. As we have observed several
times, there seem to be two primary ways in which personality
systems are organized: around some formal principle or pattern
(which is often numerical), or around some prior causal factor, either biological (genetic) or rooted in early object relations (environ-
mental). The specific categories of each system are generated either
by a formal pattern or by a causative principle, in each case interacting with observational data. To put it another way, the theorist of
type uses *either* formal principles *or* notions of causation to organize
their experience of the clients or patients with whom they work.

To integrate systems based on formal patterns boils down ultimately
to a matter of ingenuity. One looks, for example, for material in
each system that can be related to the number four, and then super-
imposes all these four-fold arrangements on each other, with everything else depending on them. Or one plays with multiplying or
dividing different numbers together, so that a three-fold and a four-
fold system combine into a twelve-fold one (as indeed happens in
astrology). This sort of integration can be thought of as a heuristic

device, perhaps, which generates new connections for evaluation; or if one takes a Jungian view that number is a fundamental organizing principle of the psyche (von Franz 1974), the process can be understood as innately meaningful.

Elements, character positions and chakras

Purely as an example of the creative possibilities, one of the authors (N.T.) – in a spirit of adventure rather than in search of any absolute truth – has constructed a synthesis of the four elements, the post-Reichian character positions, and the Ayurvedic chakras. The result is what may be termed a *map of embodiment* and its thresholds: not as a one-off event, but as a continual process of coming-into-being, moving from 'spirit' into 'matter' via elements of increasing density: Air to Fire to Water to Earth, represented as four overlapping spheres. This corresponds in a very vivid way to the developmental sequence of the character positions from head to pelvis, as discussed in Chapter 3: a process of gradual incarnation deeper into matter and deeper into the body, descending the ladder of the chakras.

But the map also highlights the developmental crisis identified by psychoanalysis as the oedipus complex: to conflate the sequence of character positions with that of the elements and chakras, one has to postulate that, when the embodiment flow reaches the genitals, and is faced with the prospect of re-entering the world through opening up to others, it sometimes fails to do so; and this failure can take more than one form. In the 'hysteric' or 'crisis' version, the energy may open out into the world, but it does so in a state of dramatized ambivalence and anxiety. In the 'phallic' or 'thrusting' version, where a person is afraid to open out (which is experienced as collapse), energy curves straight back up, rigid and self-contained within the body's energy field, into the Fire area. And in the 'psychopathic' or 'control' version, where a person is unable to trust in safe contact with others, the energy stream fails to leave the body at all but 'backs up' into the torso. Only in this way can the Reichian character sequence be brought into correspondence with the elemental pattern.

This demonstrates how the formal requirements of integrating three different systems can generate new and useful ideas about character, producing an enriched synthetic system, such as that which can be seen in summary form in Tables 7.2 and 7.3. Among other things, such a system also accounts for the 'flight from the

Table 7.2 A synthesis of three systems

	Body	Reichian segments	Chakras	Attitude axis	Character positions
Air	Head down to base of the neck	Eye, jaw and throat	Crown (sahasara), third eye (ajna) and throat (vishuddha)	Clarity/fear	Boundary, oral
Earth	Base of skull/ upper palate down to sacrum/lower belly	Throat, heart, waist and belly	Throat (vishuddha), heart (anhatta), solar plexus (manipura) and sacral (svadisthana) chakras; centred on secondary sun chakra	Desire/rage	Oral, thrusting, control, crisis
Fire	Sternum/armpits down to perineum	Heart, waist, belly and pelvis	Heart (anhatta), solar plexus (manipura), sacral (svadisthana) and base (muladhara) chakras; centred on secondary moon chakra	Joy/grief	Holding, control, crisis
Water	Navel down to soles of feet	Belly and pelvic segments	Sacral (svadisthana) and base (muladhara)	Pleasure/pain	Holding

The Air element expresses itself as about separation, distinction, distance; thus, the Boundary position ('skin', in both physical and energetic senses). Connection, communication (Air is what lies between us); thus, the Oral position. The Crown chakra brings spirit down into the clear perception of the Third Eye, enabling the Throat chakra to express and transcend its needs. Problems with this process set up issues around fear of losing boundaries – invasion/fragmentation; and fear of not communicating, not getting needs met.

The Fire element expresses itself as about appetite, enthusiasm, consuming; thus, the Oral position. Passion, excitement; thus, the Thrusting position. Assertion, achievement; thus, the Control position. Rage, survival, dominance; thus, the Crisis position. Rising, contracting energy, hot and easily frustrated. The central issue is *movement* – finding fuel for the flame. The Heart is the core of our being, and its primary expression is *love*, which can move up and out via the throat and arms, or down and out via the Sacral chakra and pelvis. The Solar Plexus chakra embodies issues of *power*, on which the heart's love may rest securely ('power for'), or which may deform and imprison love ('power over').

The Water element expresses itself as about feeling, contact, union: *yin* to Fire's *yang*; thus, the Crisis position. Water sinks and spreads, dissolving and binding charge; thus, the Holding position. Water can also be cold, contained and pent-up; thus, the Control position. With Fire (Crisis), can turn to steam; with Earth (Holding), can turn to mud. The central issue is *merging*. Fire and Water together are Union: Water, the soft side to Fire's passion, the melting heart. The Sacral chakra is the only place where three elements meet – Fire, Water Earth.

The Earth element expresses itself as about solidity, weight, definition – the completing of the embodiment process; thus, the Holding position. Only when the energy has fully grounded in Earth, meeting and merging with the flow up from the ground into the Base chakra, can it swing up and out to meet the universe.

Table 7.3 Reichian character expressed through the four elements system

---

Boundary position
The beginning of incarnation: is it safe in there? Will I be better off hovering in mid-Air? Throughout life, the energy may tend under threat to shoot back up into the head, and out of the top or back of the head altogether (dissociation). Often the edge of the Air/Fire overlap, at the base of the skull, is a block to energy moving down and up

Oral position
Fire needs to be fed; and responds to non-feeding with anger and contraction. There is a dried-up, stringy quality to Oral characters – Fire/Air. The need for feeding is in order to ground, to stay incarnated

Control position
When an experience of profound invalidation underlies later development, the incarnation stream may be unable to leave the body at all when it reaches the pelvis, but curves back up into the torso, puffing it up and bulking it out, focusing energy around the Solar Plexus and issues of power-over. This will take on the flavour of one of the front-pelvis positions: either Thrusting issues of domination, or Crisis issues of seduction

Holding position
The need to defend and contain the body contents – Earth surrounds Water, protecting and damming up feelings, thickening Water into mud

Thrusting position
The incarnation flow, turning towards the world, is met by repression; it responds by staying inside the body's own energy field, streaming straight up into the Fire element, like a second spine, or a caricature of an erect phallus

Crisis position
Water–Fire: steamy, tending to thicken! Also, the incarnate version of spirit itself, firewater, *aqua vitae*. The final threshold to full incarnation: once individuated, we seek to merge again

---

politicized pelvis', referred to above, by showing this flight actually occurring in the body energy itself. The formal patterning provides a new context for the causal reasoning of the post-Reichian approach.

Integrating causal systems

Integrating causal systems is more difficult than integrating form-alist ones, in that different theories of causation cannot simply be mixed together in a single pot without losing the specific features that make them interesting. To some extent, the idea that personality type is the product of early object relations, for example, is in conflict with the idea that it reflects congenital metabolic or neurological differences. The particular causality of a type system is rooted in a fundamental approach to human existence; it often reflects a specific implied politics, a position on 'human nature' (Totton 2000).

However, this conflict can be exaggerated. Opinion in a number of fields seems increasingly to be moving towards the idea of complex and multiple causation – not 'nature *or* nurture', but 'nature *and* nurture'. It is possible that this approach itself reflects an implicit politics, a pluralistic understanding of human beings as existing simultaneously within many fields of definition and causation, rather than as manifesting one specific 'essential' nature. It is our contention that within type theory similarly several causal principles can be held together in a creative tension, providing the practitioner with a rich set of possibilities in seeking an understanding of and with the client or patient.

Dangers of integration

The prospects for an integrative typology of character and personality are thus rather favourable, at least as good as the prospects are for an integrative psychotherapy in general. And how good that is, is a matter of opinion. Certainly, there are political obstacles here as well as theoretical ones, and very definite attempts by particular schools of therapy to achieve hegemony rather than integration.

It is worth raising the question, however, of whether an integrative personality typology would necessarily be a good idea. To begin with, it would strongly encourage a crude sort of realism, a belief that the categories it defined were in some simple sense reflections of how the world itself is ordered, rather than a more or less powerful grid to superimpose on our perceptions. This crude realism is always dangerous; but perhaps especially so in a field that involves categorizing and evaluating human beings. It is essential that any integrative typology be founded not only on an understanding of personality types as a creative expression of human potential, rather than as a form of damage or pathology, but also on the recognition that all typology is at best only an approximation either to individuals or to human nature in general.

A successful integrative typology would also have to grasp a set of complicated nettles around the question of group differences. How, if at all, are men's character types different from women's? How are black people's characters different from white people's? German from French? Westerners from First Nations? These questions have hardly been tackled by most of the existing typologies. The attempts that have been made, in fact, point up the difficulties of this sort of project. As we mentioned in Chapter 3, Erikson offers correlations – somewhat romantic and hard to substantiate – between the natural environment and culturally favoured character traits. Jung made various unsatisfactory pronouncements about men and women, Europeans and Orientals, and 'national character' (see Totton 2000, 18–21); while the Reichian Elsworth Baker (1980) produced a system of 'socio-political character types' where the moderate conservative 'comes closest to health' (p. 186), whereas the liberal is superficial, unstable and 'secretly rebellious against the father' (p. 171).

As all of these examples show, it is enormously difficult to discuss the differentiation of personality between groups without simply imposing one's own prejudices and predilections.

Even beyond this, however, it is possible that we may be better off as we are, with a densely populated ecology of independent or semi-independent typological microsystems. It seems reasonable to assume that every typology that survives has worked and still works well *with certain clients*, or with certain combinations of clients and practitioners: that at least on occasion, it has proved itself illuminating, has facilitated contact and communication between two people, even if, with a different combination of people, it might have been or yet be sterile and unhelpful.

In effect, this is the rationale of the current volume: that practitioners will benefit from knowing about a wide range of approaches to character and personality, and preferably from experimenting with applying several of these to their patients or clients. Doing this over time will no doubt lead to a degree of involuntary integration, a rounding of the edges and a developing 'pidgin' language that translates between the different systems. But integration need not be the goal. Each system can be used and valued in its own right and on its own terms. And as each system in turn moves spontaneously to the fore in relation to a particular person at a particular moment, so will its accompanying vision of human nature, development and purpose move to the fore. The co-existence of these different visions must surely be enriching.

Further reading

It is the intention of the Core Concepts series to provide a compact description of each of the major concepts in psychotherapy, together with extensive references, to assist in deeper exploration of the subject where interest is stirred, or necessity demands. Given the wide choice of references offered throughout this book, perhaps making it difficult for the general reader to know where to start, we here specifically commend a limited number of the texts referred to in each chapter, which we suggest will take the reader to the key authors and key issues in different psychotherapeutic traditions.

2 Character in psychoanalysis

Fenichel, O. [1941] (1989) Psychoanalysis of character, in R.F. Lax (ed.) *Essential Papers on Character Neurosis and Treatment*, pp. 169–87. New York: New York University Press.

Freud, S. (1908) *Character and Anal Eroticism*. Penguin Freud Library, Vol. 7, pp. 205–215. Harmondsworth: Penguin.

Kernberg, O. (1989a) A psychoanalytic classification of character pathology, in R.F. Lax (ed.) *Essential Papers on Character Neurosis and Treatment*, pp. 191–210. New York: New York University Press.

Liebert, R. (1989) The concept of character: A historical review, in R.F. Lax (ed.) *Essential Papers on Character Neurosis and Treatment*, pp. 46–61. New York: New York University Press.

Reich, W. (1972) *Character Analysis*. New York: Touchstone.

3 Reich and his heirs

Kurtz, R. (1990) *Body-Centered Psychotherapy: The Hakomi Method*. Mendocino, CA: LifeRhythm.

Lowen, A. (1958) *The Language of the Body*. New York: Collier Books (originally published as *The Physical Dynamics of Character Structure*).
Reich, W. (1972) *Character Analysis*. New York: Touchstone.
Totton, N. and Edmondson, E. (1988) *Reichian Growth Work: Melting the Blocks to Life and Love*. Bridport, UK: Prism Press.

4 Jungian typology

Jacobi, J. (1968) *The Psychology of C.G. Jung*. London: Routledge & Kegan Paul.
Jung, C.G. ([1921] 1971) Psychological Types, Vol. 6 of the *Collected Works of C.G. Jung*. London: Routledge & Kegan Paul.
Loomis, M.E. (1991) *Dancing the Wheel of Psychological Types*. Wilmette, IL: Chiron Publications.
Sharp, D. (1987) *Personality Types: Jung's Model of Typology*. Toronto: Inner City Books.
Von Franz, M. and Hillman, J. (1971) *Jung's Typology*. Zurich: Springer-Verlag.

5 Humanistic and research-based typologies

Clarkson, P. (1989) *Gestalt Counselling in Action*. London: Sage.
Gardner, H. (1983) *Frames of Mind*. New York: Basic Books.
Maslow, A. (1968) *Towards a Psychology of Being*, 2nd edn. New York: Van Nostrand Reinhold.
Ornstein, R. (1977) *The Psychology of Consciousness*, 2nd edn. New York: Harcourt Brace Jovanovich.
Sheldon, W.H. (1942) *Varieties of Temperament*. New York: Harper.
Stewart, I. and Joines, V. (1987) *TA Today: a New Introduction to Transactional Analysis*. Nottingham: Lifespace Publishing.

6 Transpersonal typologies

Bolen, J.S. (1984) *Goddesses in Everywoman*. New York: Harper Colophon.
Greene, L. (1977) *Relating*. London: Coventure.
Gullan-Whurr, M. (1987) *The Four Elements*. London: Century.
Heron, J. (1992) *Feeling and Personhood*. London: Sage.
Hills, C. (1977) *Nuclear Evolution*, 2nd edn. Boulder Creek CA: University of the Trees.
Storm, H. (1972) *Seven Arrows*. New York: Ballantine.
Webb, K. (1996) *The Enneagram*. London: Thorsons.
Wilber, K. (1996) *Up from Eden: A Transpersonal View of Human Evolution*. Wheaton, IL: Quest Books.

References

Abraham, K. (1923) Contributions to the theory of the anal character, *International Journal of Psycho-Analysis*, 4: 400–18.

Abraham, K. (1925) The influence of oral erotism on character-formation, *International Journal of Psycho-Analysis*, 6: 247–58.

Abraham, K. (1926) Character-formation on the genital level of libido-development, *International Journal of Psycho-Analysis*, 7: 214–22.

Alexander, F. (1930) The neurotic character, *International Journal of Psycho-Analysis*, 11: 292–311.

American Psychiatric Association (1994) *Diagnostic and Statistical Manual of Mental Disorders* (DSM IV). Washington, DC: American Psychiatric Association.

Arehart-Treichel, J. (1981) *Biotypes*. London: Star.

Armstrong, T. (1987) *In Their Own Way*. Los Angeles, CA: Jeremy Tarcher.

Arroyo, S. (1975) *Astrology, Psychology, and the Four Elements: An Energy Approach to Astrology and its Use in the Counseling Arts*. CRCS Publications.

Baker, E.F. (1980) *Man in the Trap: The Causes of Blocked Sexual Energy*. London: Collier Macmillan.

Balint, M. (1968) *The Basic Fault: Therapeutic Aspects of Regression*. London: Tavistock.

Banton, R., Clifford, P., Frosh, S., Louisada, J. and Rosenthall, J. (1985) *The Politics of Mental Health*. London: Macmillan.

Baudry, F. (1984) Character: A concept in search of an identity, *Journal of the American Psychoanalytic Association*, 32: 455–77.

Baudry, F. (1989) The evolution of the concept of character in Freud's writings, in R.F. Lax (ed.) *Essential Papers on Character Neurosis and Treatment*, pp. 23–45. New York: New York University Press.

Bennett, J.G. (1983) *Enneagram Studies*. New York: Samuel Weiser.

Bentzen, M., Bernhardt, P. and Isaacs, J. (1996–97) Waking the body ego: Parts I–IV. *Energy and Character*, 26: 1, 26: 2, 27: 1, 27: 2.

Benziger, K. (1995) *Falsification of Type*. Rockwall, TX: KBA Publications.

Benziger, K. (1996) *Physiological and Psychophysiological Bases for Jungian Concepts*. Rockwall, TX: KBA Publications.

Bergmann, M.V. (1980) On the genesis of narcissistic and phobic character formation in an adult patient: A developmental view, *International Journal of Psycho-Analysis*, 61: 535–46.

Berne, E. (1968) *A Layman's Guide to Psychiatry and Psychoanalysis*. Harmondsworth: Penguin.

Berne, E. (1973) *Sex in Human Loving*. Harmondsworth: Penguin.

Bernhardt, P. and Isaacs, J. (1997) The bodymap: A precise diagnostic tool for psychotherapy. http://www.bodynamicusa.com/Pages/Res pages/link013.html (accessed 1 May 2000).

Bick, E. (1968) The experience of skin in early object relations, *International Journal of Psycho-Analysis*, 49: 484.

Bion, W.R. (1963) *Elements of Psycho-Analysis*. London: Heinemann.

Bion, W.R. (1970) *Attention and Interpretation*. London: Tavistock.

Blos, P. (1968) Character formation in adolescence, *Psychoanalytic Study of the Child*, 23: 245–63.

Boadella, D. (1987) *Lifestreams: An Introduction to Biosynthesis*. London: Routledge & Kegan Paul.

Boadella, D. and Smith, D. (1986) *Maps of Character*. Abbotsbury: Self-published.

Bogen, J.E. (1975) Some educational aspects of hemispheric specialization, *UCLA Educator*, 17: 24–32.

Bolen, J.S. (1984) *Goddesses in Everywoman*. New York: Harper Colophon.

Bolen, J.S. (1989) *The Gods in Every Man*. San Francisco, CA: Harper & Row.

Bopp, J., Bopp, M., Brown, M. and Lane, P. (1984) *The Sacred Tree*. Lethbridge, AL: Four Worlds Development Press.

Boy, A.V. (1989) Psychodiagnosis: A person-centered perspective, *Person-Centered Review*, 4(2): 132–51.

Boyesen, G., Boyesen, M-L., Boyesen, E. *et al.* (1980) *Collected Papers of Biodynamic Psychology*, Vols 1 and 2. London: Biodynamic Psychology Publications.

Bozarth, J. (1998) *Person-centered Psychotherapy: A Revolutionary Paradigm*. Ross-on-Wye: PCCS Books.

Bratherton, W.J. (1998) The collective unconscious and primordial influences in gender identity, in I. Alister and C. Hauke (eds) *Contemporary Jungian Analysis*, pp. 183–97. London: Routledge.

Brenner, C. (1959) The masochistic character: Genesis and treatment, *Journal of the American Psychoanalytic Association*, 7: 197–226.

Broverman, I., Broverman, D., Clarkson, F., Rosencrantz, P. and Vogel, S. (1970) Sex role stereotypes and clinical judgements of mental health, *Journal of Consulting and Clinical Psychology*, 34(1): 1–7.

Burland, C. (1967) *The Arts of the Alchemists*. London: Weidenfeld & Nicolson.

Bursten, B. (1973) Some narcissistic personality types, *International Journal of Psycho-Analysis*, 54: 287–300.

124   *Character and personality types*

Buss, D.M. (1991) Evolutionary personality psychology, *Annual Review of Psychology*, 42: 459–91.

Buzan, T. (1976) *Use Both Sides of Your Brain.* New York: E.P. Dutton.

Centre for Psychological Astrology (2000) *Prospectus.* London: CPA.

Chasseguet-Smirgel, J. (1974) Perversion, idealization and sublimation, *International Journal of Psycho-Analysis*, 55: 349–57.

Clarkson, P. (1989) *Gestalt Counselling in Action.* London: Sage.

Conger, J.P. (1994) *The Body in Recovery: Somatic Psychotherapy and the Self.* Berkeley, CA: Frog Ltd.

Cook, M. (1984) *Levels of Personality*, 2nd edn. London: Cassell.

Cronbach, L.J. (1990) *Essentials of Psychological Testing*, 3rd edn. New York: Harper.

Damasio, A. (1996) *Descartes' Error: Emotion, Reason and the Human Brain.* London: Papermac.

Damasio, A. (2000) *The Feeling of what Happens: Body, Emotion and the Making of Consciousness.* London: Heinemann.

Davis, W. (1997) Biological foundations in the schizoid process, *Energy and Character*, 28(1): 57–76.

Easser, B.R. and Lesser, S.R. (1965) Hysterical personality: A re-evaluation, *Psychoanalytic Quarterly*, 34: 390–405.

Erikson, E. (1959) *Identity and the Life Cycle.* New York: Norton.

Erikson, E. (1965) *Childhood and Society.* London: Penguin.

Erikson, E. (1980) *Identity and the Life Cycle.* New York: Norton.

Ernst, F. (1973) Psychological rackets in the OK Corral, *Transactional Analysis Journal*, 3(2): 19–23.

Eysenck, H.J. (1991) Dimensions of personality: 16, 5 or 3? Criteria for a taxonomic paradigm, *Personality and Individual Differences*, 12: 773–90.

Fabricius, J. (1994) *Alchemy.* London: Diamond Books.

Fenichel, O. ([1941] 1989) Psychoanalysis of character, in R.F. Lax (ed.) *Essential Papers on Character Neurosis and Treatment*, pp. 169–87. New York: New York University Press.

Fenichel, O. (1945) *The Psychoanalytic Theory of Neurosis.* New York: Norton.

Ferguson, M. (1973) *The Brain Revolution.* New York: Taplinger.

Fink, B. (1995) *The Lacanian Subject: Between Language and Jouissance.* Princeton, NJ: Princeton University Press.

Fisher, S. and Greenberg, R.P. (1977) *The Scientific Credibility of Freud's Theories and Therapy.* New York: Basic Books.

Fodor, J. (1998) The trouble with psychological Darwinism, *London Review of Books*, 20(2): 11–13.

Fordham, F. (1966) *An Introduction to Jung's Psychology.* Harmondsworth: Penguin.

Foucault, M. (1974) *The Archaeology of Knowledge.* London: Tavistock.

Frager, R. (ed.) (1994) *Who am I? Personality Types for Self-Discovery.* London: Aquarian.

Freud, A. (1936) *The Ego and Mechanisms of Defence.* London: Hogarth Press.

Freud, S. (1905) *Three Essays on the Theory of Sexuality*. Penguin Freud Library, Vol. 7, pp. 31–169. Harmondsworth: Penguin.

Freud, S. (1908) *Character and Anal Eroticism*. Penguin Freud Library, Vol. 7, pp. 205–215. Harmondsworth: Penguin.

Freud, S. (1914) *On Narcissism*. Penguin Freud Library, Vol. 11, pp. 59–97. Harmondsworth: Penguin.

Freud, S. (1920) *Beyond the Pleasure Principle*. Penguin Freud Library, Vol. 11, pp. 269–338. Harmondsworth: Penguin.

Freud, S. (1923) *The Ego and the Id*. Penguin Freud Library, Vol. 11, pp. 339–407. Harmondsworth: Penguin.

Freud, S. (1931) *Libidinal Types*. Penguin Freud Library, Vol. 7, pp. 359–65. Harmondsworth: Penguin.

Freud, S. (1939) *Moses and Monotheism*. Penguin Freud Library, Vol. 13, pp. 237–396. Harmondsworth: Penguin.

Fromm, E. (1947) *Man for Himself*. Greenwich, CT: Fawcett Premier Books.

Fromm, E. (1960) *The Fear of Freedom*. London: Routledge & Kegan Paul.

Fromm, E. (1973) *The Anatomy of Human Destructiveness*. New York: Holt Rinehart & Winston.

Frosch, J. (1964) The psychotic character: Clinical psychiatric considerations, *Psychiatric Quarterly*, 38: 81–96.

Gale, A. and Eysenck, M.W. (eds) (1992) *Handbook of Individual Differences: Biological Perspectives*. Chichester: Wiley.

Gardner, H. (1983) *Frames of Mind*. New York: Basic Books.

Gardner, R. (1970) *Evolution Through the Tarot*. London: Rigel Press.

Gardner, R. (1974) *The Tarot Speaks*. London: Tandem.

Gazzaniga, M. (1970) *The Bisected Brain*. New York: Appleton-Century-Crofts.

Gergen, K.J. (1994) *Reality and Relationships: Soundings in Social Construction*. Cambridge, MA: Harvard University Press.

Gitelson, M. ([1954] 1989) Theoretical problems in the analysis of normal candidates, in R.F. Lax (ed.) *Essential Papers on Character Neurosis and Treatment*, pp. 409–27. New York: New York University Press.

Glover, E. (1926) The neurotic character, *International Journal of Psycho-Analysis*, 7: 11–30.

Goldberg, L.R. (1993) The structure of phenotypic personality traits, *American Psychologist*, 48: 26–34.

Goulding, R. and Goulding, M. (1972) New directions in Transactional Analysis, in H.S. Sager and C.J. Kaplan (eds) *Progress in Group and Family Therapy*, pp. 105–134. New York: Brunner/Mazel.

Greene, L. (1977) *Relating*. London: Coventure.

Grey, A. (1992) Society as destiny – Fromm's concept of social character, *Contemporary Psychoanalysis*, 28: 344–63.

Grossinger, R. (1986) *Embryogenesis: From Cosmos to Creature, the Origins of Human Biology*. Berkeley, CA: North Atlantic Books.

Gullan-Whurr, M. (1987) *The Four Elements*. London: Century.

Guntrip, H. (1968) *Schizoid Phenomena, Object Relations and the Self*. London: Hogarth Press.

Hall, N. (1980) *The Moon and the Virgin*. London: The Women's Press.

Heron, J. (1992) *Feeling and Personhood*. London: Sage.

Heron, J. (1998) *Sacred Science: Person-centred Inquiry into the Spiritual and the Subtle*. Ross-on-Wye: PCCS Books.

Hillman, J. (1980) *Egalitarian Types Versus the Perception of the Unique*. Zurich: Spring Publications.

Hillman, J. (1996) *The Soul's Code: In Search of Character and Calling*. New York: Random House.

Hillman, J. and Ventura, M. (1992) *We've had a Hundred Years of Psychotherapy – and the World's Getting Worse*. San Francisco, CA: Harper Collins.

Hills, C. (1968) *Nuclear Evolution*. Boulder Creek, CA: University of the Trees.

Hills, C. (1977) *Nuclear Evolution*, 2nd edn. Boulder Creek, CA: University of the Trees.

Hinshelwood, R.D. (1997) The elusive concept of 'Internal Objects' (1934–1943): Its role in the formation of the Klein group, *International Journal of Psycho-Analysis*, 78: 877–97.

Houzel, D. (1990) The concept of psychic envelope, in D. Anzieu (ed.) *Psychic Envelopes*, pp. 27–58. London: Karnac Books.

Issacharoff, A. (1991) Issues in character and resistance analysis (panel presentation), *Contemporary Psychoanalysis*, 27: 720–1.

Jacobi, J. (1968) *The Psychology of C.G. Jung*. London: Routledge & Kegan Paul.

Jaynes, J. (1976) *The Origins of Consciousness in the Breakdown of the Bicameral Mind*. Boston, MA: Houghton-Mifflin.

Johnson, R.A. (1993) *The Fisher King and the Handless Maiden: Understanding the Wounded Feeling Function in Masculine and Feminine Psychology*. New York: HarperCollins.

Johnson, S.M. (1985) *Characterological Transformation*. New York: W.W. Norton.

Joines, V. (1986) Using Redecision Therapy with different personality adaptations, *Transactional Analysis Journal*, 16(3): 152–60.

Jones, E. ([1918] 1977) Anal-erotic character traits, in E. Jones (ed.) *Papers on Psychoanalysis*, pp. 413–37. London: Karnac.

Joseph, B. (1989) *Psychic Equilibrium and Psychic Change*. London: Routledge.

Jung, C.G. ([1921] 1971) Psychological Types, Vol. 6 of the *Collected Works of C.G. Jung*. London: Routledge & Kegan Paul.

Jung, C.G. ([1935] 1986) *Analytical Psychology: Its Theory and Practice (The Tavistock Lectures)*. London: Ark.

Jung, C.G. ([1953] 1969) Psychology and Alchemy, Vol. 12 of the *Collected Works of C.G. Jung*. London: Routledge & Kegan Paul.

Jung, C.G. (1956) Symbols of Transformation, Vol. 5 of the *Collected Works of C.G. Jung*. London: Routledge & Kegan Paul.

Jung, C.G. ([1958] 1970) Psychology and Religion: West and East, Vol. 11 of the *Collected Works of C.G. Jung*. London: Routledge & Kegan Paul.

Jung, C.G. ([1959] 1968) The Archetypes and the Collective Unconscious, Vol. 9, Part I of the *Collected Works of C.G. Jung*. London: Routledge & Kegan Paul.

Jung, C.G. (1962) Commentary, in R. Wilhelm (ed. and trans.) *The Secret of the Golden Flower*, pp. 81–137. London: Routledge & Kegan Paul.

Jung, C.G. (1963) *Mysterium Coniunctionis*, Vol. 14 of the *Collected Works of C.G. Jung*. London: Routledge & Kegan Paul.

Jung, C.G. (1978) *Man and His Symbols, Conceived and Edited by Carl Jung*. London: Picador.

Kahler, T. (1970) *Transactional Analysis Revisited*. Little Rock. Human Development Publications.

Kazdin, A.E. (1986) Comparative outcome studies of psychotherapy: Methodological issues and strategies, *Journal of Consulting and Clinical Psychology*, 54: 95–105.

Keleman, S. (1985) *Emotional Anatomy*. Berkeley, CA: Center Press.

Kelley, C.R. (1979) Character and radix functions, *The Radix Journal*, 1: 4.

Kernberg, O. (1989a) A psychoanalytic classification of character pathology, in R.F. Lax (ed.) *Essential Papers on Character Neurosis and Treatment*, pp. 191–210. New York: New York University Press.

Kernberg, O. (1989b) Character analysis, in R.F. Lax (ed.) *Essential Papers on Character Neurosis and Treatment*, pp. 211–29. New York: New York University Press.

Khan, M.M.R. (1966) Role of phobic and counterphobic mechanisms and separation anxiety in schizoid character formation, *International Journal of Psycho-Analysis*, 47: 306–12.

Kingsland, K. (1973) A course in human communication, unpublished paper delivered at the Centre for Human Communication, Torquay, Devon.

Kingsland, K. and Kingsland, V. (1976) *Complete Hatha Yoga*. London: David & Charles.

Kingsland, K. and Kingsland, V. (1977) *Hathapradipika*. Torquay: Grael Communications.

Kline, P. (1972) *Fact and Fantasy in Freudian Theory*. London: Methuen.

Kohut, H. (1971) *The Analysis of the Self*. New York: International Universities Press.

Kohut, H. (1977) *The Restoration of the Self*. New York: International Universities Press.

Kraepelin, E. (1917) *Lectures on Clinical Psychiatry*. New York: William Wood.

Kurtz, R. (1990) *Body-Centered Psychotherapy: The Hakomi Method*. Mendocino, CA: LifeRhythm.

Lakoff, G. (1987) *Women, Fire and Dangerous Things: What Categories Reveal about the Mind*. Chicago, IL: University of Chicago Press.

Laplanche, J. and Pontalis, J.B. (1988) *The Language of Psychoanalysis*. London: Karnac.

Levine, P.A. (1997) *Waking the Tiger: Healing Trauma*. Berkeley, CA: North Atlantic Books.

128   *Character and personality types*

Liebert, R.S. (1989) The concept of character: A historical review, in R.F. Lax (ed.) *Essential Papers on Character Neurosis and Treatment*, pp. 46–61. New York: New York University Press.

Lilly, J. (1973) *The Centre of the Cyclone*. London: Paladin.

Loomis, M.E. (1991) *Dancing the Wheel of Psychological Types*. Wilmette, IL: Chiron Publications.

Lowen, A. (1958) *The Language of the Body*. New York: Collier Books (originally published as *The Physical Dynamics of Character Structure*).

Lowen, A. (1976) *Bioenergetics*. Harmondsworth: Penguin.

MacCuish S., Patel, M. and Jones, J. (1998) *Walking with the Bhagavad Gita*. Bilston, UK: Life Foundation Publications.

Maslow, A. (1968) *Towards a Psychology of Being*, 2nd edn. New York: Van Nostrand Reinhold.

Maslow, A. (1971) *The Farther Reaches of Human Nature*. New York: Viking.

Mattoon, M.A. (1981) *Jungian Psychology in Perspective*. New York: Free Press.

Mearns, D. and Thorne, B. (1992) *Person-centred Counselling in Action*. London: Sage.

Metzner, R. (1981) Towards a reformulation of the typology of function, *Journal of Analytical Psychology*, 26(1): 33–48.

Mindell, A. (1985) *River's Way: The Process Science of the Dreambody*. London: Arkana.

Mindell, A. (1992) *The Leader as Martial Artist: An Introduction to Deep Democracy*. San Francisco, CA: Harper.

Mishra, R.S. (1959) *Fundamentals of Yoga*. New York: The Julian Press.

Moore, R. and Gillette, D. (1990) *King, Warrior, Magician, Lover*. San Francisco, CA: Harper.

Myers, I.B. (1962) *The Myers-Briggs Type Indicator*. Palo Alto, CA: Consulting Psychologists Press.

Nichols, S. (1984) *Jung and Tarot: An Archetypal Journey*. York Beach, ME: Samuel Weiser.

O'Hanrahan, P. (1999) *Enneagram Tools for Personal Growth*. Trumansburg, NY: The Crossing Press.

Ornstein, R. (1977) *The Psychology of Consciousness*, 2nd edn. New York: Harcourt Brace Jovanovich.

Ornston, D.G. (ed.) (1992) *Translating Freud*. London: Yale University Press.

Painter, J.D. (1986) *Deep Bodywork and Personal Development*. Mill Valley, CA: Bodymind Books.

Palmer, H. (1991) *The Enneagram: Understanding Yourself and the Others in Your Life*. New York: HarperCollins.

Palmer, H. (1994) Sacred Type: The Nine Enneagram Personalities, in R. Frager (ed.) *Who am I? Personality Types for Self-Discovery*. London: Aquarian.

Pelletier, K.R. (1978) *Towards a Science of Consciousness*. New York: Dell.

Penfold, P.S. and Walker, G.A. (1984) *Women and the Psychiatric Paradox*. Buckingham: Open University Press.

Perls, F. ([1955] 1975) Gestalt therapy and human potentialities, in J.O. Stevens (ed.) *Gestalt Is*, pp. 1–8. New York: Bantam.

Perls, F., Hefferline, R.F. and Goodman, P. (1973) *Gestalt Therapy: Excitement and Growth in the Human Personality*. Harmondsworth: Penguin.

Perry, B.D., Pollard, R.A., Blakley, T.L., Baker, W.L. and Vigilante, D. (1995) Childhood trauma, the neurobiology of adaptation and use-dependent development of the brain: How states become traits, *Infant Mental Health Journal*, 16(4): 271–91.

Pervin, L.A. (ed.) (1990) *Handbook of Personality: Theory and Research*. New York: Guilford Press.

Pett, J. (2000) Gay, lesbian and bisexual therapy and its supervision, in D. Davies and C. Neal (eds) *Therapeutic Perspectives on Working with Lesbian, Gay and Bisexual Clients*, pp. 54–72. Buckingham: Open University Press.

Pierrakos, J. (1987) *Core Energetics: Developing the Capacity to Love and Heal*. Mendocino, CA: LifeRhythm.

Pinker, S. (1998) *How the Mind Works*. London: Allen Lane.

Poster, M. (1978) *Critical Theory of the Family*. London: Pluto Press.

Prigogine, I. and Stengers, I. (1985) *Order Out of Chaos: Man's New Dialogue with Nature*. London: Flamingo.

Quenk, N.L. (1993) *Beside Ourselves: Our Hidden Personality in Everyday Life*. Palo Alto, CA: Consulting Psychologists Press.

Reich, W. (1972) *Character Analysis*. New York: Touchstone.

Reich, W. (1973) *The Function of the Orgasm*. London: Souvenir Press.

Reich, W. (1975) *The Mass Psychology of Fascism*. Harmondsworth: Penguin.

Revelle, W. (1995) Personality processes, *Annual Review of Psychology*, 46: 295–328.

Rogers, C. (1956) *Client-Centered Therapy*. Boston, MA: Houghton-Mifflin.

Rohr, R. (1990) *Discovering the Enneagram: An Ancient Tool for a New Spiritual Journey*. New York: Crossroad.

Rose, H. and Rose, S. (eds) (2000) *Alas, Poor Darwin: Arguments Against Evolutionary Psychology*. London: Jonathan Cape.

Rothwell, J. (1994) *Control of Human Voluntary Movement*. London: Chapman & Hall.

Rowan, J. (1993) *The Transpersonal: Psychotherapy and Counselling*. London: Routledge.

Rowan, J. (1996) Integration as transformation, *Self and Society*, 24(3): 4–14.

Rudhyar, D. (1972) *The Astrological Houses: The Spectrum of Individual Experience*. New York: Doubleday.

Samuels, A. (1985) *Jung and the Post-Jungians*. London: Routledge & Kegan Paul.

Schafer, R. (1979) Character, ego-syntonicity, and character change, *Journal of the American Psychoanalytic Association*, 27: 867–91.

Schermer, B. (1989) *Astrology Alive! Experiential Astrology, Astrodrama, and the Healing Arts*. New York: HarperCollins.

Sharaf, M. (1983) *Fury on Earth: A Biography of Wilhelm Reich*. New York: St. Martin Press.

Sharp, D. (1987) *Personality Types: Jung's Model of Typology*. Toronto: Inner City Books.

Sheldon, W.H. (1942) *Varieties of Temperament.* New York: Harper.

Shlien, J.M. (1989) Boy's person-centered perspective on psychodiagnosis, *Person-Centered Review*, 4(2): 157–62.

Singer, J. (1995) *Boundaries of the Soul: The Practice of Jung's Psychology*, 2nd edn. Bridport, UK: Prism Press.

Singer, J. and Loomis, M.E. (1984) *The Singer–Loomis Inventory of Personality (SLIP)*. Palo Alto, CA: Consulting Psychologists Press.

Southgate, J. (1980) Basic dimensions of character analysis, *Energy and Character*, 11(1): 48–67.

Springer, S. and Deutsch, G. (1985) *Left Brain, Right Brain*. New York: Freeman.

Stein, M.H. (1969) The problem of character theory, *Journal of the American Psychoanalytic Association*, 17: 675–701.

Steiner, J. (1993) *Psychic Retreats*. London: Routledge.

Stern, D. (1985) *The Interpersonal World of the Infant*. New York: Basic Books.

Stewart, I. and Joines, V. (1987) *TA Today: A New Introduction to Transactional Analysis*. Nottingham: Lifespace Publishing.

Storm, H. (1972) *Seven Arrows*. New York: Ballantine.

Storr, A. (1973) *Jung*. London: Fontana.

Sun Bear and Wabun (1980) *The Medicine Wheel: Earth Astrology*. New York: Prentice-Hall.

Suzuki, S. (1973) *Zen Mind, Beginner's Mind*. New York: Weatherhill.

Totton, N. (1998) *The Water in the Glass: Body and Mind in Psychoanalysis*. London: Rebus Press.

Totton, N. (2000) *Psychotherapy and Politics*. London: Sage.

Totton, N. and Edmondson, E. (1988) *Reichian Growth Work: Melting the Blocks to Life and Love*. Bridport, UK: Prism Press.

Trevarthen, C. (1987) Split-brain and the mind, in R. Gregory (ed.) *The Oxford Companion to the Mind*, pp. 740–7. Oxford: Oxford University Press.

Van der Kolk, B.A., McFarlane, A.C. and Weisaeth, L. (eds) (1996) *Traumatic Stress: The Effects of Overwhelming Experience on Mind, Body and Society*. London: Guilford Press.

von Franz, M. (1974) *Number and Time: Reflections Leading Towards a Unification of Psychology and Physics*. London: Rider.

von Franz, M. and Hillman, J. (1971) *Jung's Typology*. Zurich: Springer-Verlag.

Ware, P. (1983) Personality adaptations (doors to therapy), *Transactional Analysis Journal*, 13(1): 11–19.

Webb, J. (1980) *The Harmonious Circle*. London: Thames & Hudson.

Webb, K. (1996) *The Enneagram*. London: Thorsons.

Wehr, D.S. (1987) *Jung and Feminism: Liberating Archetypes*. London: Routledge.

Wheelwright, J.B., Wheelwright, J.H. and Buehler, J.A. (1964) *Jungian Type Survey: The Gray-Wheelwrights Test*. San Francisco, CA: Society of Jungian Analysts of Northern California.

Wilber, K. (1995) *Sex, Ecology and Spirituality: The Spirit of Evolution*. Boston, MA: Shambhala.

Wilber, K. (1996) *Up from Eden: A Transpersonal View of Human Evolution*. Wheaton, IL: Quest Books.

Wilden, A. (1972) *System and Structure: Essays in Communication and Exchange.* London: Tavistock.

Wilkinson, R. (1967) *The Temperaments in Education.* Fair Oaks, CA: St George Publications.

Winnicott, D.W. ([1949] 1975) Mind and its relation to the psyche-soma, in *Through Paediatrics to Psychoanalysis: Collected Papers,* London: Karnac. pp. 243–54.

Winnicott, D.W. ([1960] 1965) Ego distortion in terms of true and false self, in *The Maturational Processes and the Facilitating Environment.* London: Hogarth Press.

Woolger, J.B. and Woolger, R.J. (1989) *The Goddess Wheel.* New York: Ballantine.

Young-Eisendrath, P. and Wiedemann, F. (1987) *Female Authority: Empowering Women through Psychotherapy.* London: Guilford Press.

Zuercher, S. (1992) *Enneagram Spirituality: From Compulsion to Contemplation.* South Bend, IN: Ave Maria Press.

Index

Note: The main subjects of chapters (e.g. psychoanalysis, transpersonal therapies) are indexed only as they occur outside that chapter.

von Franz, M., 11, 55, 59, 61, 67, 89, 115

Ware, P., 77–8
Webb, K., 101, 106
Wehr, D.S., 67, 105
Wilber, K., 98–100

Wilden, A., 111–12
Wilkinson, R., 90
Winnicott, D.W., 29, 37
Woolger, R., 103–5

yoga, 98
Young-Eisendrath, P., 67, 105

THE THERAPEUTIC ENVIRONMENT
CORE CONDITIONS FOR FACILITATING THERAPY

Richard J. Hazler and Nick Barwick

Psychology bookshelves are filled with texts on different theories of how to do therapy and why one specific theory will work better than all the others. Yet the fact is research proves over and over again that *all* theories can work under the right conditions. This book takes a unique look at the specifics of those conditions that are facilitative to all forms of therapy, and how they are identified in different theories.

The diverse experiences and viewpoints of an American humanistic therapist and a British psychodynamic therapist are brought together to explore the essential conditions needed for therapy to succeed. Extensive use of first-hand examples and thorough academic support combine to create vivid text, a sound theoretical base and practical therapeutic applications. The opening chapters draw on substantial research evidence which suggests that all theoretical approaches are equally effective in the hands of good therapists. It proposes that an important factor contributing to this effectiveness is the environment in which therapy is practised. Three central chapters give in-depth explorations of the unique ways in which the broad theoretical orientations of psychodynamic, existential-humanistic, and cognitive-behavioural deal with the philosophy, labelling, function, perspective and implementation of a facilitative environment. A concluding chapter synthesizes information from these diverse orientations to identify core commonalities and critical differences between how therapists from different theoretical persuasions develop common understandings, maintain working client relationships and regulate their personal involvement in therapy.

Contents

160pp   0 335 20282 9 (Paperback)   0 335 20283 7 (Hardback)

INTERNALIZATION
THE ORIGINS AND CONSTRUCTION OF INTERNAL REALITY

Kenneth C. Wallis and James L. Poulton

The process of internalization is fundamental to all forms of psycho-therapy. It is difficult to see how any healing process is meaningful unless the one to be healed 'takes home' some element of the cure. How else may a 'cure' take place unless it is *internalized*? This book surveys the development of concepts pertaining to the processes by which an individual's internal world comes into being. The core concepts of internalization – identification, incorporation and introjection, which heavily influenced the evolution of psychoanalytic schools, illustrate the commonalities and differences between a wide variety of psychotherapeutic paradigms. Through an examination of representative proponents of the four major sub-divisions of psychotherapeutic schools – psychoanalysis, cognitive-behavioural, humanistic/existential and family-systems – the authors show how internalizing concepts and principles shed light on the theory and practice of psychotherapy.

The universality of the human condition and the humanitarian goal of psychotherapeutic healing pose an ethical mandate to search for common threads of meaning across the paradigmatic spectrum. *Internalization* addresses that mandate through elucidation of concepts as applied to a variety of theoretical contexts. Through this comparative method, the authors hope to contribute to the self-examination of the psychotherapeutic enterprise, and to elucidate the mechanisms underlying therapeutic efficacy.

Contents
Core concepts of internalization – Internalization in psychoanalytic schools – Internalization in behaviourism and cognitive-behavioural schools – Internalization in family, systems and group schools – Internalization in humanistic/existential schools – The validity of internalization theory: thesis and antithesis – References – Index.

208pp   0 335 20305 1 (Paperback)   0 335 20306 X (Hardback)

THE SELF AND PERSONALITY STRUCTURE

Paul M. Brinich and Christopher Shelley

- What is the self and its relationship to personality theories?
- How do the central schools of psychotherapy conceptualize the self?

The *self* is a notoriously difficult and at times obscure concept that underpins and guides much psychotherapy theory and practice. The corollary concept of personality is fundamentally linked to the concept of the self and has provided theorists and researchers in psychology with a more coherent set of principles with which to explicate the personal and attributional aspects of the self. The authors come from two quite separate schools of depth psychology (psychoanalytic and Adlerian) and provide an overview of the self and how it is conceptualized across the psychotherapies within various theories of personality. In addition to outlining some of the philosophical and historical issues surrounding the notion of selfhood, the authors examine classical and developmental models of psychoanalytic thought that implicitly point to the idea of self. The authors also outline Kohut's psychoanalytic *self psychology* in addition to Adlerian and other post Freudian, Jungian and post-Jungian, cognitive, humanistic, and existential contributions to the self and personality structure.

Contents

c.128pp   0 335 20563 1 (Paperback)   0 335 20564 X (Hardback)

EMOTIONS AND NEEDS
THE CORE CONCERNS OF PSYCHOTHERAPY

Dawn Freshwater and Chris Robertson

It could be argued that in this age of anxiety we do not face emotion and need in honesty and consciousness, either as therapists or clients. Instead, emotions have become the Cinderella of the psyche. They manifest everywhere: in political outbursts, in socializing and in private conflicts. Their repression is marked by the rapid increase we have seen in depression and suicide, manic behaviour and in desperate pleas to 'Lady Lottery'.

In *Emotions and Needs* the authors attempt to bring the phenomenon of emotional needs to the foreground. Emotions and needs are perceived as core concerns and feature centrally in all psychotherapies. What is less acknowledged is that psychotherapy *is* the natural history of emotions. Indeed the whole rationale of psychotherapy begins with unconscious symptoms (physical or emotional) which the logical mind has failed to fathom. Despite their centrality and their lack of logical reasoning it is the thinking structures which attempt to make emotions intelligible.

As an alternative to classifying modalities of psychotherapy (and the way in which they understand needs and emotions) by their author, era or underpinning philosophy, *Emotions and Needs* focuses on the emotional patterning of psychotherapy. In particular the authors explore need and emotion in relation to what patients bring to therapy and what subsequently facilitates effective engagement with need and emotion in the therapeutic alliance.

Contents
Core concepts of needs and emotions – Physical birth: pre-ego needs and emotions – Psychological birth: the heat of the relationship – Mid-life transition: psychotherapy as courtly love – Integrating needs and emotions: emotional intelligence – Conclusions – Further reading – References – Index.

c.128pp   0 335 20801 0 (Paperback)   0 335 20802 9 (Hardback)

TRANSFERENCE AND PROJECTION
MIRRORS TO THE SELF

Jan Grant and Jim Crawley

This book focuses on how transference and projection are used by therapists of different theoretical persuasions. The volume describes, defines and demonstrates clinical applications of transference and projection in therapy and then shows how the major schools of psychotherapy conceptualize and deal with such clinical phenomena. A core feature of the book is how therapists with different approaches can utilize such clinical phenomena effectively. It focuses on how transference and projection are used by therapists as 'mirrors to the self' – reflections of the client's internal world and core ways of relating to others. An important feature of this book is how it integrates differing psychotherapeutic approaches. Clinical material from the authors' clinical practices bring to life the major principles of working with transference and projection.

Contents

An introduction to transference – Projection and projective identification – Transference and projection: the origins – Developments in transference theory: psychodynamic psychotherapies – Cognitive-behavioural therapies and transference phenomena – The humanistic-existential and experiential therapies and transference – Transference and projection in couples and family therapy – Working with the transference clinically – References – Index.

c.128pp   0 335 20314 0 (Paperback)   0 335 20315 9 (Hardback)